A GOOD BRAIN WASHING

Black and White Version

*Take Control of Your Mind with a
Personalized Recording*

Georganne P. Bickle

Combined Book and Workbook

© February 2008/2012 by Georganne P. Bickle

Published by Create Space, North Charleston, SC

First Printing, November 2012

Printed in the United States of America

For workshops and seminars, please contact the author at the following:

Georganne P. Bickle
P O Box 30646
Phoenix, AZ 85046
info@gbickle.com

ISBN: 1481077945

ISBN-13: 978-1481077941

Cover designed by James E. Ruiz, roccruiz@gmail.com

Copyrights /Permissions:
All illustrations and extended texts are used with permission of the original author or organization. Detailed reference lists are available at the end of every chapter and constructed according to the Publication Manual of the American Psychological Association 5th edition.

For my beautiful and intelligent daughter Jessica, who gave me a reason to live, taught me how to love, and motivates me to push myself higher.

Disclaimer

The material presented in this book is a result of research compiled over the previous three years. In order to provide readers with a solid reasoning as to why this works, I have included quotes and references to numerous research studies and articles. I have taken the utmost care to cite sources accurately both in the text and in the reference section of each chapter.

After years of suffering intense mental and emotional pain, I believe the Lord Jesus Christ led me to this discovery as an answer to my prayers. I have personally used this tool for the past decade. In the introduction, I describe this process in detail.

This is **NOT** and has nothing to do with the following: New Age, Transcendental Meditation, Hypnosis, Name It and Claim It Movement, Prosperity Gospels, Scientology, etc.

I am not so naïve as to believe that this is anything new or unique. I am aware there are other organizations and authors with similar tools and mind training methods available for public purchase. However, **this book is a direct result of my personal experience**. At no time, in no manner shape, or form, have I attempted to copy or plagiarize anyone's commercial training products, tools, or recordings, etc. I have seen this work in my life and I sincerely believe this works for anyone willing to use it and apply it to their life.

"What you are is God's gift to you, what you become is your gift to God."

Hans Urs von Balthasar (1905-1988), *Prayer*
(one of the most important theologians of the 20th century)

Acknowledgements

To some people this book may seem like a little pebble in the road of published texts, especially for those who are experienced in creating skilled masterpieces. For me, this book is a truly great miracle.

There are many people to whom I owe a tremendous amount of gratitude for helping me to keep trudging the rough and rocky road of life when it would have been easier to end the pain inside and just give up.

First, I would like to thank my family and friends for their continued love and support throughout all of the difficult years. Especially my mother and my best friend Kitty, who stood by me and covered me with her prayers. Special thanks to Gerianne and Kathy for your love, wisdom, and guidance. You set an excellent example of hard work and dedication in your passion for helping others. You are true professionals. Thank you to Jessica and Dan for taking time to read the manuscript and give me your advice and suggestions. I am proud of both of you and love you deeply.

I am extremely blessed to have been guided by some of the wisest and most wonderful people in the world before they left this earth to walk the streets of gold with Jesus. I want to honor the memories of the following people: Les Echols, Dottie Shore, Mama Ruth, Margie Simpson, Black Wally, and my precious sponsor Yvonne Porter – all of whom told me what I needed to hear, not wanted I wanted to hear. Also, Father Martin, I am grateful for his 12-step visit to my home. He planted the seed of hope in my mind. He gave my mother the much-needed reassurance that I might live to get sober and clean someday.

To the women in my veteran PTSD group, thank you for your constant love and support. You are some of the bravest and most courageous women I have ever known. In the face of adversity, you stand tall and proud ever pushing forward to overcome the horrendous crimes committed against you.

Thank you to Joyce and Dave Meyer who have saved my life and my sanity more times than I can count. You are a powerful reflection of Christ and continue to be a source of strength and wisdom in my life.

Thank you to all of my wonderful professors at Regent University. You helped me achieve what I thought was impossible. You continue to shine brightly with the love of Christ. I could not have asked for a better learning environment or better friends and mentors.

To all the doctors, nurses, and staff at the Carl T. Hayden VAMC, thank you for always treating me with value and dignity. Your compassion and caring are immensely helpful to my healing process and continued quality of health.

Thank you Dr. Kenneth Harris for taking valuable

time to read my scribbling and helping me to understand the brain's processes. Thank you for your wonderful insight and expert instruction.

A very special thank you to Karen Miller, LCSW/LISAC. You have continued to share your love, support, and wisdom with me over the past nine years. Even when I pushed your tolerance levels to the maximum and probably got on your last nerve. You always gently brought me back to the present moment and gave me a smile. Thank you for teaching me how to "breathe."

Most importantly, thank you Jesus for never leaving my side and always giving me your unconditional love. You brought order and sanity out of the chaos and destruction. You are my Savior, husband, mentor, best friend, and constant companion. Thank you for allowing me to discover a tool to share with others that restores hope and helps dreams become possible.

"For I know the plans I have for you, declares the LORD, plans to prosper you and not to harm you, plans to give you hope and a future."

Jeremiah 29:11 (NIV)

TABLE OF CONTENTS

Note

The purpose of this book and workbook is for use as a **supplement** to your primary spiritual and/or recovery materials. It is **not for use as a replacement or substitution** for:

- attendance at church, meetings or support groups
- appointments with mental health professionals or medical professionals
- Bible or religious text
- basic recovery Text
- Or any other materials that are important and vital to your continued spiritual growth, recovery, and healing process.

There is no way to predict how quickly you can see the results from using your personal recording. Some people may begin to notice a change in a few days, whereas for others, it may take a few months or years. For those of us who have experienced deeper levels of trauma, long-term abuses, or long-term addictions - a longer period of healing is required. Have patience and persistence. This tool of using a personal recording helps you if you continue to use it on a regular ongoing basis.

This book is intentionally written in a conversational tone vs. a scholarly format in order for any reader regardless of education or background, to feel comfortable in applying the information in this book and workbook to their life.

Introduction

My main motivation for writing this book and workbook is that I have seen major changes in my life and more importantly the way I think, act, and react to life's challenges. Where once I was considered by many to be hopeless (including my own view), I am now a healthy functioning and responsible member of society. Did it solve all of my problems? No. Was it a miracle cure? No. However, I found a tool that worked to effectively change my thinking patterns and subsequently improve the quality of my faith, recovery, and healing process. I believe God led me to discover this tool to ease my pain and suffering and to help me move forward. Since this tool, this personalized recording, has worked so effectively to help change my life, I know that it can work for anyone willing to use it on a daily basis.

To be clear, I am not a doctor, neurologist, scientist, or researcher. I do have a limited medical background from working as a nurse in the military many, many moons ago. However, I find the subject of neuroscience one of the most interesting and make a regular practice of reading anything I can find on brain research as often as possible. The question of why we think the way we do and how the brain processes information is both intriguing and fascinating. Neuroscience is filled with constant new discoveries.

For purposes of this introduction, I explain how I discovered this tool of creating a personalized recording. Where once I felt like my mind was flying down the tracks of life like a runaway train with no brakes, using this tool on a daily basis has allowed me to be back at the controls and to enjoy a peace and stability that I have never known.

There are times in life when we get to the point of needing to solve a difficult problem and we stumble onto something incredible. We can be pulled in so many directions that either our time is overly in demand or we feel ourselves shrinking under the weight of stress. We desperately search for a solution that provides relief, preferably a healthy solution. I was experiencing just such a time in my life when I discovered this tool.

As a child in school, I could ace all of my tests without ever opening a book to study. As long as I paid attention in class and listened to what the teacher had to say, A's came easy for me. However, as an adult faced with numerous problems, it became evident that my concentration had flown out the window. When I attempted to learn anything new, it was as difficult as attempting to climb Mt. Everest with a broken leg.

When I returned to school in middle age, I had to read and reread, make outlines, and spend hours trying to retain information. I needed to find a way to learn a great deal of information in a short time. I was taking so many notes in my classes that my finger seemed to have a permanent dent from holding the pencil. There were so many pages to review by the end of the day that I felt overwhelmed and wondered how I would ever remember so much information. I heard other people talking about the effectiveness of tape recording lectures and how easy it was to remember the high points after listening to their recording several times.

I decided to take it one-step further. I started recording all of my notes, terms, lessons, or anything that I thought was important. I listened to my recordings in the car, while doing housework and laundry, and before bedtime. I began to notice that if I was listening to my own voice on tape - my memory was much sharper than if I was listening to someone else such as a teacher giving a lecture. My grades started to improve and tests became easier thus allowing me to finish in a shorter time. The mental stress of being back in school after so many years began to lessen and I found it easier to keep up with a full time schedule.

About this same time, I started receiving affirmation lists from my counselors and becoming aware of affirmations from Bible teachers and authors like Joyce Meyer. I started hearing stories of how affirmations could make a difference in the recovery process, improve self-esteem, and strengthen your faith. I decided to put the two together. I began recording my own affirmations and listening to them as often as I could. Next, I added some of my favorite scriptures.

At this point, I did not really believe any lasting change was possible because I had been a literal mess for so long. It seemed like a life filled with daily chaos and crisis was the only normal one. Although I was sober and clean and had been for a number of years, and an active member of a church, it felt like something was missing. I had worked the steps numerous times – writing each one out and sharing it with my sponsor. I attended more meetings than I could count and worked in service commitments. I worked with newcomers, read the Bible daily, prayed constantly, etc., but stability and peace of mind seemed just beyond my grasp.

However, I became aware that when I listened to my recording on a regular basis – I felt better. My thoughts were more rational. I started to feel calmer during the day. When I flew into my rages, they were closer to the midline instead of being so intense. When I felt depressed, it was also closer to the midline instead of being so low that I could not get off the couch for days at a time.

Over a period of several years of trial and error, I came up with a recording of meditations and affirmations that were personal to me. My list was a combination of statements that fit my life and described what I wanted my life to look like. I noticed that Native American flute music helped me to relax and feel peaceful, so I played it in the background when recording my affirmations. I made a habit of listening to my recording every night and every morning.

As I watched my life begin to improve, I wanted to know why. Why was this working for me when numerous attempts at therapy had failed? Why was this creating stability in my life when I had begged God for years to change me emotionally and mentally? Why was my focus improving when none of the medications that my doctors had given me had produced any positive results? Why were my flashbacks and nightmares starting to disappear and become less frequent? I had to have answers. I began to study books on the brain and thinking patterns. I researched medical studies and read everything I could find on sound and the way the brain processes sounds, especially that of one's own voice. I began to see that God had designed our brains to work in a certain way. I saw that when my brain had locked on to certain patterns of thinking and behaving, any attempt to change those patterns had been met with unconscious resistance and failure.

My brain was used to one set pattern of thinking and reacting. It did not matter what I tried or how much I wanted to change it, my brain would always return to that familiar pattern. The only way I found to break that pattern was to start listening to my recording on a regular basis – every day and night. There are physical reasons why hearing your own voice on a recording is completely different from hearing someone else's voice. Listening to your own voice just before you fall asleep at night affects your mind in such a powerful way that it creates lasting change in your actions and reactions throughout your waking hours.

In recovery meetings, we often hear the saying "act as if ...," the same principle holds true for a successful personalized recording. You must describe the life you want before it is a reality. I began by recording the verbal picture of the type of person I wanted to be and what my life could look like, as if everything had already changed. Though it took some time, the statements began coming true.

One example that I discuss further in Chapter 4, is that I had always wanted to own my own home. Given my inability to hold a job, past credit history, and low credit score, this was completely impossible for me. However, I am here to tell you that today - I own my own home and have for the past 3 years. Another advantage is that since I bought this home, I have never been late or missed one mortgage payment. Miracles happen! This only occurred because I followed the directions that God gave me in putting this dream on my daily recording as if it already happened, but concluding it with "Thy Will, not Mine Be Done." I listened to my recording every night and every morning.

Using this tool has worked for me and is continuing to work for me, a once hopeless society throwaway! That is why I know this can work for you if you give it a chance. What do you have to lose? Like they say in meetings, "Try it for 90 days and if it doesn't work, we will refund your misery."

A GOOD BRAIN WASHING

Take Control of Your Mind with a Personalized Recording

Combined Book and Workbook

A GOOD BRAIN WASHING

"Idea" by Idea go / Free Digital Photos.net[1]

"As A Man (or Woman) Thinketh, So Is He (or She)"

Proverbs 23:7 (KJV)

A GOOD BRAIN WASHING

CHAPTER 1:
WHY DO OUR BRAINS NEED WASHING?

The term "brainwashing" is discussed in detail in Chapter 3, but for our purpose here, we are talking about getting rid of negative or destructive thinking and replacing it with positive statements that add to a mental and emotional healthy life. We are actually talking about renewing the mind. This is not about giving anyone else control of your mind. It is a way for you to follow God's plan and take control over your own thoughts. This is a way to take control over your life. This provides a way to see the dreams God has planted in your heart and mind become a reality.

When faced with the question of why we need to wash our brains or renew our minds, one of the most important reasons is the fact that thoughts are real things. Thoughts create energy, in us, around us or depending on the circumstance - both. Of course, there are a multitude of reasons for the need to wash our brains or renew our minds on a daily basis, but we are going to 'Keep It Simple Sweetie' (KISS - I prefer 'sweetie' to 'stupid' as it is less demeaning). If you have attended any recovery meetings, you have no doubt heard some of the speakers referring to the 'old tapes' running in their heads. What they are talking about are the lies that others have told us over the years and the lies we tell ourselves.

One of my favorite recovery speakers was Bob E. He used to tell the story about waking up to see his mind sitting on the headboard in the form of a vulture waiting for him. His mind said something like, "Oh I'm glad you're awake, there are a few things I want to talk to you about. Remember that bump on your knee? It's no bump, it's cancer! You have to undergo chemotherapy and you will lose your hair. You are going to die! Now that you have cancer and are going to die, you will lose your job. And without a job and no hair, your wife is going to leave you and file for divorce. Without a job, and alimony to pay, you are going to lose your house. So you have cancer, have lost your job, your wife, and your house, so what the heck are you going to do now?" He's only been awake for 5 minutes!

This is a good example of the way our minds can blow things out of proportion. This type of thought pattern is not based in reality, yet we often take thinking patterns like this as pure gospel. We allow them to create fear, dread, and/or terrible emotional pain to torture us throughout our every waking minute. This is the most important reason to wash out our brain or renew our mind on a daily basis. I do not want to live my life with such horrible thinking controlling me.

Some of you are probably saying, 'well I don't have those problems, I've never been in recovery or any program. Okay, just so no one feels left out, we can review a few statistics on the following pages. These numbers are a good representation of people today and the problems that are affecting many around the world. If you are honest with yourself, you may find at least one statement that applies to you or your life.

Current Statistics

The Department of Veterans Affairs experts believe that PTSD occurs in[1]:

- 11 – 20% of Veterans that served in Operation Iraqi Freedom and Operation Enduring Freedom

- 10% of Desert Storm Veterans

- 30% of Vietnam Veterans

The figures above do not include current or former service members who have never sought treatment or individuals who may have sought treatment through private therapists, counselors, or doctors.

For Combat and Sexual Trauma related events, the percentages are significantly higher.

The National Alliance on Mental Illness (NAMI) reports the following statistics on their website[2]:

- The National Institute of Mental Health reports that one in four adults-approximately 57.7 million Americans-experience a mental health disorder in a given year

- The U.S. Surgeon General reports that 10 percent of children and adolescents in the United States suffer from serious emotional and mental disorders that cause significant functional impairment in their day-to-day lives at home, in school and with peers.

- The World Health Organization has reported that four of the 10 leading causes of disability in the US and other developed countries are mental disorders. By 2020, Major Depressive illness will be the leading cause of disability in the world for women and children.

- Bipolar disorder affects 5.7 million American adults, approximately 2.6 percent of the adult population per year.

- Anxiety disorders, which include panic disorder, obsessive-compulsive disorder (OCD), post-traumatic stress disorder (PTSD), generalized anxiety disorder, and phobias, affect about 18.1 percent of adults, an estimated 40 million individuals.

- An estimated 5.2 million adults have co-occurring mental health and addiction disorders.

- Suicide is the eleventh leading cause of death in the U.S. and the third leading cause of death for ages 10 to 24 years.

- Without treatment the consequences of mental illness for the individual and society are staggering: unnecessary disability, unemployment, substance abuse, homelessness, inappropriate incarceration, suicide and wasted lives. The economic cost of untreated mental illness is more than 100 billion dollars each year in the United States.

The Rape, Abuse & Incest National Network (RAINN) reports the following statistics[3]:

- 44% of victims are under age 18

- 80% are under age 30

- Every 2 minutes someone in the U.S. is sexually assaulted
- Each year there are 207,754 victims of sexual assault

- 54% of sexual assaults are not reported to police

- 97% of rapists will never spend a day in jail
- Approximately 2/3 of assaults are committed by someone known to the victim

- 38% of rapists are a friend or acquaintance

- Victims include men - About 3% of American men or 1 in 33 have experienced an attempted or completed rape in their lifetime

- 2.78 million men in the U.S. have been victims of sexual assault or rape

The National Coalition Against Domestic Violence (NCADV) reports the following statistics[4]:

- One in every four women will experience domestic violence in her lifetime

- An estimated 1.3 million women are victims of physical assault by an intimate partner each year

- Most cases of domestic violence are never reported to police
- Boys who witness domestic violence are twice as likely to abuse their own partners and children when they become adults

- 30% to 60% of perpetrators of intimate partner violence also abuse children in the household

- The cost of intimate partner violence exceeds $5.8 billion each year. $4.1 billion of which is for direct medical and mental health services

The National Council on Alcoholism and Drug Dependence (NCADD) reports[5]:

- 22.6 million people (9.2%) of the U.S. population ages 12 and older) have an alcohol or drug problem

- 2.4 million adolescents have an alcohol or drug problem
- 50% of adults have a family member with alcoholism

- Approximately 1 in 4 children under 18 live in a family with alcoholism, and many more live in a family with drug addiction.
- Alcoholism is the 3rd leading lifestyle-related cause of death in the nation.

- Alcohol and drug dependence costs the nation over $276 billion a year, resulting principally from lost productivity and increased health care spending.

According to the American Psychological Association (APA) [6]:

- Two in five (41%) employed adults report that they typically feel stressed out during the workday

- Less than six in ten (58%) report that they have the resources to manage work stress

- Less than half of employees (46%) report being satisfied with the growth and development opportunities offered by their employer

- Less than half of employees report feeling that they are receiving adequate monetary compensation (48%)

- Nearly one-third of employed adults (32%) report that they are having difficulty balancing work and family life

- Job stress costs U.S. businesses an estimated $300 billion per year through absenteeism, diminished productivity, employee turnover and direct medical, legal and insurance fees

The National Center for Complimentary and Alternative Medicine (NCCAM) which is a branch of the National Institute of Health reports[7]:

- Over 1.6 million American adults use some form of complimentary and alternative medicine – aka "CAM" to treat insomnia or trouble sleeping

These are significant reasons why we need to wash our brains or renew our minds on a daily basis. To be clear, the recording tool described in this book is not offered as a cure all. There is no promise or statement made here that this tool is a cure for any or all of the above problems.

However, it has been proven to help ease the suffering and emotional pain of individuals who may believe they have any of the above conditions, if (emphasis on IF), you use it on a daily basis. **You only get out of it, the equivalent of the effort you are willing to put into it.** You must follow directions and use your recording according to the directions outlined in Chapter 4, in line with the way God designed our brains to work.

There is no quick fix, no magic pill or no easy out. This is a supplemental tool, not a replacement for your own therapy, counseling, consultations with your doctor, or spiritual advisors, etc.

Childhood Influences

There are several important areas of influence on the way our minds process information that we can change to experience a better quality life. From the time we are conceived in our mother's womb and our brains begin to develop, there is an internal listening device that starts to record everything we hear. Medical studies have proven that babies can hear and remember certain things from the time they were in their mother's womb. In one case Dr. Murray (2002) notes, "… the study showed foetuses [fetuses] had both short and long-term memories."[8] Even more recently another study reported by Dirix et.al (2009):

> Fetuses were observed to have a short-term (10-min) memory from at least 30 weeks GA onward, which also appeared independent of fetal age. In addition, results indicated that 34-week-old fetuses are able to store information and retrieve it 4 weeks later.[9]

In my own life, I tested this theory when I was

pregnant with my daughter. Every night before I went to sleep, I would place my hands on my stomach and sing to my unborn child the song Amazing Grace.[10] After she was born, I would again sing Amazing Grace to her whenever she was cranky or crying and could not sleep. Her eyes would stare up at me with a look of recognition and she would instantly become calm and peaceful. Within no time, she was in a deep sleep. In fact, I repeated this process many times throughout her childhood when she was troubled and every time she heard me singing Amazing Grace she would experience calmness and peace.

In the article *Babies Remember Womb Music,* the BBC News reported a study that proved babies can "remember and prefer music that they heard before they were born over 12 months later." During the study, one mother reported that before her daughter was born she played Ella Fitzgerald music while taking her bath every evening. This was her way to relax and de-stress. After her daughter was born, she would play Ella Fitzgerald whenever her daughter became cranky. The effect was that her daughter remembered the music from the womb and would relax into a calm mood.[11]

Toby MacDonald wrote, directed, and produced a film in 2005 called *In The Womb*, which aired on the National Geographic Channel, wherein he notes reactions of the fetus to music. When the fetus recognized music that had a fast beat, the fetus appeared to be dancing and when slow music was played, a calming effect on the fetus was observed.[12]

The problem is that we are not born with an internal filter to discard the negative statements we hear and hold on to only the positive statements. The messages that run through our brains have the power to shape who we are, what we do, and what we believe about the world around us and ourselves. In some cases, the negative messages received in childhood can take a lifetime to overcome.

For example, look at the child who grows up in a mixed environment of both positive and negative statements. The child may have one loving parent who is always encouraging and praising the child, but the other parent is always insulting and demeaning the child. The child's brain receives both positive and negative messages about his or her identity. By the time the child grows into a teenager, he or she experiences a constant mix of self-confidence and self-doubt. The child most probably swings from one extreme to the other – acting out good behavior in one area and then acting out bad behavior in another.

It is a well-known fact that the negative messages we receive from others in our childhood stick with us on a subconscious level. These negative messages are often the root cause of irrational behavior and thoughts that plague many adults throughout their lifetime.

My own experience is proof of this principle. Even though both of my parents acted loving, supportive, nurturing, and affectionate – the emotional and physical abuse that I experienced by daycare providers when I was five years old, left lasting effects. This one horrible event etched a deep scar in my emotions and my mind. My parents never knew what occurred and I never told them until many years into adulthood. My mind told me it was all my fault – that I was bad and deserved it or it would not have happened to me. As a result, I went through childhood with a mixture of positive and negative messages about myself swirling around in my brain. I was a straight 'A' student, but could not behave as expected in social situations. Later in life, I was super sensitive to any comments made about my body. If my boyfriend made any comments about my body or appearance, even in fun, it sent me into a rage and an intense argument would follow. I had no idea why I was reacting that way.

Today, I understand that my behavior was a result of a mixed influence of positive and negative messages. I felt good about myself in some areas and hated myself with regard to other areas of my life. The horrible statements made to me before, during, and after the abuse at the day care center would run through my mind over and over – "You are dirty", "You are bad", "No man will ever want to touch you", "You are stupid", "You are ugly" etc.

Peers are another powerful source of the messages

we believe about ourselves and that run through our minds constantly. How many times have we seen one child being singled out on the playground for being a little different from the others? That child is often ridiculed and humiliated to the point of tears. My daughter had a high IQ that became very noticeable when she entered elementary school at age six. She understood complicated words, used them in the right context, and could carry an intelligent conversation with adults. Her classmates used to accuse her of "talking funny" because she used words that they did not comprehend. She came home from school very upset on several occasions. It took a great deal of time and effort to help her understand that she was not the problem. With young children, the pain of rejection by others produces a long list of negative messages that run through the brain or the mind repeatedly.

Messages like:

> You're ugly
> You're stupid
> You're dumb
> You're weird
> You dress funny
> You talk funny
> You have buck teeth
> Four eyes (kids with glasses)
> Railroad tracks or tin teeth (kids with braces)
> You're fat or You're too skinny
> You're an idiot

You're such a nerd
Can't you ever do anything right?

…along with hundreds of other insults and name-calling.

Additionally, the experiences we encounter during the teenage years can deeply affect us throughout our lifetime and be much more complicated than friends we have in elementary school. Guzman (2007) points out that, "Friendships that emerge during adolescence tend to be more complex, more exclusive, and more consistent than during earlier childhood."[13] These complex and exclusive relationships can carve out deeper scars on the mind and emotions because as teenagers the need to be accepted is often the most important controlling thought in the mind and emotions.

How many times have we seen teenagers change their hair or their clothes or get piercings because they just want to fit in and be accepted? There are clicks of Goth, Emo, Preppies, Jocks, Stoners, Punkers, Geeks, Ravers, etc, each with their own hairstyles, dress code, and slang. Many turn to drugs and alcohol to shut off their insecurities and painful feelings because the thoughts running through their minds are so overwhelming.

Self-Talk

Self- Talk is another highly motivating factor in why we need to wash out our brains or renew our minds on a daily basis. Have you ever listened to the things you say to yourself? I mean really listened! If someone else said the things we say to ourselves, we would instantly be in fighting mode or at the very least cut that person out of our lives and never speak to them again.

When I started paying attention to the things I said to myself, I was a bit shocked. Would I say those things to my best friend? No. Would I say those things to my enemy? Maybe, but highly doubtful. Yet here I am saying that to myself. No wonder I had such a low sense of self-esteem and felt worthless. I heard myself saying things like:

> You stupid idiot, you did it again.
> What were you thinking, when you got dressed this
> morning? You look like a jerk.
> That was a really dumb thing to say, no wonder you
> don't have any friends.
> Awkward! You are the queen of creating awkward
> moments.
> No wonder he left you. You don't deserve to be
> loved.
> No wonder you are divorced, you are the worst lover
> he's ever had.
> No one is ever going to forget how stupid you acted
> tonight.
> Ugh! Your hair looks like crap, you should have
> never cut it. Why couldn't you just leave it alone.
> You are weird, really weird. That's why you don't fit

in anywhere.

How lame! You can't even tell a story the right way. Even when you try to sound intelligent – you sound stupid so just don't say anything.

I can't believe you, why do you always think of a good comeback when it's too late to say it.

You always say the wrong thing

You have got to be the worst mother that ever lived.

All the problems your daughter has ever had are all your fault.

No one will ever understand you – so don't try.

You are going to fail anyway – you always do!

You are too fat.

You are too old.

You missed your chance.

And on and on – ad nauseam!

In addition to the self-image and personality lies we tell ourselves, there are obsessive lies that we create which cause anxiety and depression or impulsive behavior that we always end up regretting. In my adult life, I had a very difficult time acquiring any type of stability in any area of my life. One of main areas this instability surfaced was on the job. I would start a new position with a great deal of excitement, filled with hope about the endless possibilities. Yet, after a few months, I would get so bored that I would start telling myself:

I can't stand this anymore, this job is so boring

> I can't stand this place, I am so restless at being
> locked in here all day
> I need to be working outside
> I need to work at home, then I would feel satisfied

Once those thoughts began to dominate my thinking, it was all over. Within a few days or weeks, I would quit my job. Financial trouble would follow. There was not enough money to pay the bills. I would lose my apartment and that meant that my daughter and I would have to move yet again.

Relationships were another area that I would tell myself these same types of lies.

> He just doesn't understand
> I am better off without him
> He is not the guy I was looking for
> Surely, there is someone better out there for me
> If I stay with him, I'll miss the right one

Sure enough, once these thoughts started to run through my every waking moment, it would not be long before I was breaking up or running away and the relationship was over. I missed a great relationship with a good man – several times – due to this destructive thinking pattern.

Media Messages

Not only are we affected by our experiences and by the influence of the people around us, but we are also affected by society and media influences. As small children we are given toys to play with that, create an image of what we should be like.

Most little girls of my generation all had Barbie dolls. Barbie was the little doll with a perfect figure, blue eyes, and blonde hair. The problem was that when I looked in the mirror, I did not look anything like Barbie, so my brain immediately assumed there was something lacking in me – something wrong with me. After all, she was perfect! Most of you have probably heard of the Real Life Barbie Doll women. Shapouri (2008) reported that:

> Sarah Burge has broken the world record for cosmetic procedures (she's had more than 100) in an effort to turn herself into a living doll. Her actions trump the previous record-holder, our own stateside "Barbie" Cindy Jackson who also says her surgery obsession is spurred by her desire to look like the iconic Mattel toy.[14]

The same thing was true for many little boys of my generation. They were given G.I. Joe figures. G.I. Joe was a male doll with a perfect physical stature, formed strong muscles, and very handsome. He was tough, strong, and a hero. How many little boys looked in the mirror and saw that they did not look like that image and then decided that there was something lacking in them? How many of them took dangerous steroids to try to attain the G.I. Joe body? According to CNN.com (2007),

"In the United States, about 3 million people use anabolic steroids — one in four of these steroid users started as a teenager, and one out of every 10 is a teenager."[15]

A dear friend of mine once said that she wished she could burn every book on Cinderella. Often times, girls grow up thinking they have to be a Cinderella and find Prince Charming to live happily ever after. My two favorite books growing up were "The Ugly Duckling" (because I could relate) and "Cinderella". I felt like the ugly duck and wanted to be the swan. Of course, my mind decided there was definitely something wrong with me because I never changed into the swan. No matter how hard I tried to be like Cinderella, I usually ended up acting like one of the wicked stepsisters. There were times when I thought I had found Prince Charming, but he usually turned out to be a wolf in disguise. The point is that we can form negative messages about ourselves even from an innocent source. It depends on what we tell ourselves and what we end up believing is true.

Media influences are powerful sources when it comes to developing a self-image. Clark (2009) states:

> Researchers have suggested that media may influence the development of self-esteem in adolescents through messages about body image. Television, movies, magazines, and advertisements present images that promote unrealistic expectations of beauty, body weight,

and acceptable physical appearance. Efforts to sell an image that adheres to certain standards of body weight and size may be a catalyst for eating disorders suffered by some adolescents.[16]

The media equally influence not only children, but also teenagers and adults. Thousands of advertising campaigns, which cost thousands of dollars, are targeted at specific audience types to sell specific products based on behavior patterns and beliefs.

Commercials, Television shows, and Movies are filled with beautiful women and handsome men. They are always the winners, the heroes, the ones who received all the attention and all the praise. What about the characters who are a little fat, a little skinny, or a little nerdy? They are the ones who are usually the brunt of a joke, the ones being cast aside, or the ones being laughed at and made fun of at every turn. Also, notice that in almost every instance the bad guy, the criminal, or the evil one was the farthest from considered good looking. What kinds of negative messages do these portrayals send to our brain – especially when we look in the mirror?

How many normal everyday looking people do you find in the magazines? Most ads feature young and gorgeous women and well built handsome young men. How many of us look like that? I remember when Twiggy was the top model and famous all over the world in the mid 1970s. Everyone I knew wanted to look like Twiggy, which for most of us was next to impossible. My friends and I went on starvation diets only to end up sick and missing school. This reinforced the message that I just was not good enough.

Today young women want to be like their favorite singer, actress, or model. While young men want to be like their favorite singer, actor, or athlete. What happens when they look in the mirror and do not match up to their favorite star? What messages run through their brain? As a result of all the media focus on being and appearing as the perfect woman or man, our thoughts review a long list of our faults to prove that we can never be good enough. This adds to our insecurities, our fears, and to low self-esteem. Often this type of thinking over a period of time can result in unhealthy behaviors and/or mental illness such as anorexia and/or bulimia, alcoholism, drug addiction, obsessive-compulsive disorder, etc.

Negative Thinking Cycles

When we experience any kind of abuse in our lives, we have a completely new set of negative messages to deal with. We blame ourselves for putting ourselves in that position or bringing out the worst in someone else. In the case of sexual traumas, our first impulse is to tell ourselves that we deserve it because we are bad, guilty, or at fault. If we were not it would not have happened in the first place. This of course, it a complete set of lies. No one deserves to be raped or abused in any way whatsoever!

We find ourselves endlessly stuck in a negative cycle of drawing destructive relationships to ourselves repeatedly and wonder why. We meet a new man or a new woman and think to ourselves "this time will be different," but within a short while this new partner turns out to be the same – verbally and/or physically abusive and then we wonder how we ended up in this type of relationship yet again. Or going to the other extreme, we tell ourselves that relationships never work out and we isolate. We stop dating and run the other way every time we meet a new man or a new woman. We tell ourselves that all men or women are bad or that we are damaged goods and that no would want me if they really knew me. If we do meet that rare quality man or woman and begin to experience a healthy relationship, we cannot handle it. Most of the time, unconsciously, we end up sabotaging the relationship or running away and forming all kinds of excuses to justify our behavior.

When we experience traumatic events (accidents, violence, combat, etc.) or are the victims of a crime (rape, mugging, attacks, etc.) our minds replay the event repeatedly. We continually chide ourselves for not being somewhere else, "if only I had…" On any given day, we may be enjoying a movie or time with our friends or some other activity when suddenly something triggers a recurrence of the trauma. Our palms begin to sweat, our breathing is labored, and we experience a sense of panic rising up in our throats and we feel like the trauma is happening all over again or is about to happen. Or worse, we continually experience vivid nightmares of the traumatic event that can continue for months or years.

After I lost several children before birth, I would dream that I was in a large room filled with clouds so thick I could barely see my hand in front of my face. From off in the distance I would hear a child let out a blood curdling scream, "Mommy, mommy help me they are trying to kill me, help me mommy". I would race in the direction of the voice as hard and as fast as I could. Suddenly, the child's voice would be in another direction screaming the same thing, so I would run that way. This would go on and on until I would wake up in bed shaking and in a cold sweat, barely able to breathe.

When a person suffers or has suffered from any one or a combination of - mental illness, sexual trauma, sexual abuse, alcoholism, or any other type of addiction, a common result is to become locked into a negative thinking pattern affecting each area of life. This negative thinking cycle, often at the subconscious level, has the effect of manifesting all kinds of chaos and trouble in the sufferer's life repeatedly. Even with a strenuous effort in counseling and a recovery program, the desire to achieve a quality life and experience a deep level of peace and contentment can remain out of reach for some people. The sufferer is nagged by the continual feeling that "something" is wrong, but they cannot find the answer to what that "something" is.

The "something" lies in the fact that for years they have been essentially brainwashing the mind to believe that life is and always will be painful. When life becomes enjoyable it conflicts with the core message in the subconscious mind. The person unintentionally creates a negative or painful scenario to reinforce the message that life is painful. For example, if you drove down the same dirt road for years with your tires hitting the same exact place in the dirt, over time your tires would wear a deep rut in the road surface. This is exactly what happens in the brain, over time the deep rut of negative thinking becomes the only natural and comfortable one to follow.

The only way to reverse this negative thinking pattern is to begin to renew the mind into a positive thinking cycle. Just as we "train" children to walk and talk, we have to "train" our minds to respond to challenges and problems in a positive way. There are specific guidelines to follow in reversing the damage of negative thinking patterns and specific "do's" and "don'ts" to follow in establishing a positive thinking cycle according to the way God designed our brains to work.

That is what this recording tool does. It helps you to create new patterns in your brain to respond to situations differently. By teaching your brain to think and respond in a new way, you act and react to situations differently. This process is similar to putting yourself on autopilot. In the past, the auto pilot response follows a negative track due to the way you trained your brain to respond. After using this recording for a period of time, you train your brain to follow a positive track and respond to situations automatically in a positive healthy mind set.

You must be persistent and patient !!!

Establishing a new way of thinking and reacting takes time and repetition. For example if you are 35 years old, you need to realize that this is an effective tool, but what took you 35 years to do – could take months or years to undo.

A common belief in addiction recovery is it takes at least 2 months of sober/clean time for every year of active addiction to restore emotional/mental growth. If you drank and used drugs for 10 years, it can take 20 months of sober/clean time to start growing emotionally and mentally. My life is an example. I began drinking alcohol at 12 years old and drug use at 14 years old. I drank and used for 26 years. It took me 52 months (over 4 years) of continuous sober/clean time to begin to grow emotionally and mentally. I had been trying to emotionally and mentally respond to my adult life and responsibilities as a 12 to 14 year old child. It simply did not work; my life was screwed up and chaotic!

Your brain recovery works the same way. The negative tracks and cycles in your brain are deeply embedded. The best way and the fastest way to change those negative paths into positive paths are to listen to your own recording every night and every morning.

The effectiveness depends on your effort to personalize your recording to your specific problems. No two people are the same, so a "cookie cutter" format does not work. You must look at your own life and apply it specifically to your healing process. If you are not sure what to include on you recording, it is strongly suggested that you sit down with your counselor, therapist, pastor, sponsor, or other spiritual advisor and make a list of affirmations that apply specifically to your life. This is covered in more detail in Chapter 4.

Chapter 1 - References

1. U.S. Department of Veterans Affairs, National Center for PTSD (2012). *Understanding PTSD booklet.* http://www.ptsd.va.gov/PTSD/public/pages/fslist-ptsd-overview.asp

2. National Alliance on Mental Illness (2009). *Mental Illnesses: What is Mental Illness, Mental Illness Facts.* http://www.nami.org/Content/NavigationMenu/Inform_Yourself/About_Mental_Illness/About_Mental_Illness.htm

3. Rape, Abuse & Incest National Network (2009). *Statistics.* http://www.rainn.org/statistics

4. National Coalition Against Domestic Violence (2009). *Domestic Violence Facts.* http://www.ncadv.org/files/DomesticViolenceFactSheet%28National%29.pdf

5. National Council on Alcoholism and Drug Dependence (2009). *NCADD Facts and Information.* http://ncadd.org/index.php/for-the-media/press-kit

6. American Psychological Association (2012). http://www.apa.org/news/press/releases/phwa/workplace-survey.pdf and http://www.apa.org/helpcenter/labor-day.aspx

7. National Center for Complimentary and Alternative Medicine, CAM for Insomnia or Trouble Sleeping (2006). http://nccam.nih.gov/news/multimedia/audio/091806clip.htm

8. Murray, B. (2002). *The Brain: Babies Can Learn in the Womb.* Uplift Program, Health and News Research, Health Topics.

9. Dirix, C., Nijhuis, J., Jongsma, H., & Hornstra, G. (2009). Aspects of fetal learning and memory. *Child Development, 80*(4), 1251-1258. doi:10.1111/j.1467-8624.2009.01329.x.

10. Newton, John (1725-1807). Amazing Grace. Liberty Lyrics, maintained by Jon Roland of the Constitution Society. (Original date 1998 – last updated 2011). http://www.constitution.org/col/amazing_grace.htm

11. BBC News, Health. *Babies remember womb music.* (2001, Jully 11) http://news.bbc.co.uk/2/hi/health/1432495.stm

12. McDonald, Toby (Writer, Producer, Director). (2005). *National Geographic Channel's In The Womb* [Film]. Inbar Mayaan, Embryo Project Encyclopedia (2010) ISSN: 1940-5030. http://embryo.asu.edu/view/embryo:128550

13. Guzman, M.R.T. de (2007). *Friendships, Peer Influence, and Peer Pressure During the Teen Years.* Neb Guide G1751, University of Nebraska-Lincoln. http://www.ianrpubs.unl.edu/epublic/live/g1751/build/g1751.pdf?redirected=true

14. Shapouri, Beth. (2008). Wacky Beauty News of the Day: Woman Breaks World Record to Look Like Barbie [Electronic Version]. *Glamour Beauty, Girls in the Beauty Department, Daily Beauty Blog, October 29.* http://www.glamour.com/beauty/blogs/girls-in-the-beauty-department/2008/10/wacky-beauty-news-of-the-day-w.html

15. *Performance enhancing drugs and your teen athlete* (2007). CNN.com, Health Library, Mayo Clinic.com. http://www.cnn.com/HEALTH/library/SM/00045.html

16. Clark, Laura B. (2009). *Media Influence on Children.* Education Encyclopedia, State University.com. http://education.stateuniversity.com/pages/2212/Media-Influence-on-Children.html

Illustrations

1. Idea by Idea go/ Free Digital Photos.Net http://www.freedigitalphotos.net/images/Environmental_Concep_g389-Idea_p24841.html

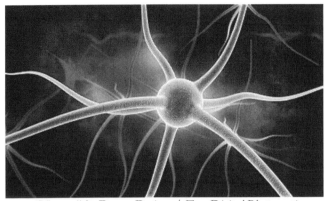

"Neuron" by Dream Designs / Free Digital Photos.net[1]

"Thank you for making me so wonderfully complex! Your workmanship is marvelous."

Psalm 139:14 (NLT)

Chapter 2:
How God designed our Brains to work

How exactly do our brains work? This is a question that scientists and researchers have been striving to answer since the beginning of man. According to "The Secret Life of the Brain – History of the Brain Video Series" [2002], the first written document about the brain originated thousands of years ago:

4000 B.C. The first known writing on the brain is found in ancient Sumerian records from this period. The anonymous writer describes the euphoric mind-altering sensations caused by ingesting the common poppy plant.[1]

For a history of writings about the brain, see Appendix A.

The human brain is a complicated and mysterious frontier filled with vast uncharted territories. There are numerous research teams around the world conducting medical studies on the brain. A recent Google search on the internet of the word "brain" returned 635 million results and the words "brain research" returned 438 million. An advanced search using the words "brain research", limited to educational web sites only (.edu) - produced in excess of 4 million results. These numbers give you a good idea of the extreme complexity of the brain and its functions.

The purpose of this chapter is to provide readers with a basic knowledge of the brain and its anatomy. The highly complex processes that take place during thoughts and emotions would be very difficult to explain in a single setting. Keeping that fact in mind as you read, understand that this section provides you with a limited basic overview of what is occurring in your brain and body at the same time as you have a thought and/or emotion.

The human brain weighs only about 3 pounds and is responsible for controlling both conscious and unconscious processes. The brain is at work 24 hours a day, 7 days a week and is described by some as a super computer. In a similar way to a computer, the output largely depends on the input. If we load up our computers with faulty programs, the results are disastrous. Similarly, when we load up our minds with negative or destructive messages the output is never beneficial to ourselves or anyone in our environment.

The "brain" is generally understood to be the center of our intelligence, the mass of nerves and tissue that control information both inside and outside of our physical bodies. The "mind" is generally understood to be the center of our memory, consciousness, and control for thinking, feeling, reasoning, etc.

Where exactly is the mind located within the brain structure? There is not one location. The mind is made up of many processes within the brain and at times, depending on the focus of the mind, can involve numerous structures and parts of the brain. For instance, Searle (1992) in the, "The Problem of Consciousness" believes that "brain processes cause conscious processes."[3] He believes that arrays of neurons work together in different parts of the brain, combining and interpreting stimuli (information), internal and external; to create awareness from the time we wake up in the morning until we go to sleep at night.[2]

Merriam-Webster (2012) defines "consciousness" as "the quality or state of being aware especially of something within oneself; the upper level of mental life of which the person is aware as contrasted with unconscious processes."[3] For example, a conscious thought occurs when looking at a pot of boiling water. My thoughts produce a full awareness that the action of sticking my finger into the boiling water has a direct consequence of pain and a burn injury to my finger that may require medical attention.

The word "unconsciousness (unconscious)" is defined as "not knowing or perceiving: not aware; not marked by conscious thought, sensation, or feeling." Merriam-Webster (2012) further defines this process as:

> The part of mental life that does not ordinarily enter the individual's awareness yet may influence behavior and perception or be revealed (as in slips of the tongue or in dreams).[4]

An example of an unconscious process is the simple act of breathing. I do not need to remind myself to breath, I just do it automatically without thinking about it. The important point to note in the explanation above are the words "may influence behavior or perception." When we suffer from PTSD or addictions, our unconscious thoughts have a strong influence on our behavior and our perceptions. This is highly evident during a PTSD related flashback or nightmare. Our unconscious mind believes the past event is happening in the present moment and can recreate images, smells, and emotions in our conscious mind with the result of reliving the past experience in the present moment. Our conscious awareness of the present moment and our present surroundings fade and are replaced by the event from our past. This is discussed in more detail toward the end of this chapter, but for now let us continue our discussion of the anatomy of the brain.

Your brain is housed in a thick protective shell made of bone called the skull or the cranium. The brain is divided into three main areas: the forebrain, midbrain, and hindbrain. The forebrain consists of the cerebrum, thalamus, and hypothalamus (part of the limbic system). The following picture shows the Cerebrum or Cortex which is the largest part of the human brain and is associated with higher brain function such as thought and action. As you can see, the Cerebrum is divided into two sides called the right and left hemispheres. The right hemisphere is associated with creativity and the left hemisphere is associated with logic abilities.

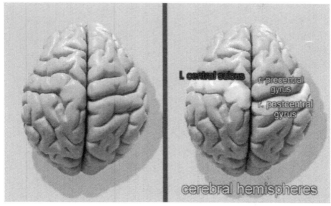

"Cerebral Hemispheres" by Pam Gregory, Tyler Junior College[2]

Dividing the two hemispheres is a type of bridge called the Corpus Callosum. In the Cerebral Hemispheres picture, this appears as the long narrow gap between the two hemispheres, but is not visible as the location would be at the bottom of the gap. The Corpus Callosum is a very thick bundle of nerve fibers. In the 18th century, it was considered the site of the soul (Maurice Ptito).[5] Communication between the two hemispheres occurs because of the Corpus Callosum. Many neuroscientists are currently studying this section of the brain to increase their understanding of these communication processes.

The Cerebrum is divided into four lobes: Frontal Lobe, Parietal Lobe, Temporal Lobe, and Occipital Lobe.

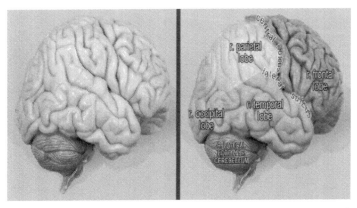

"Cerebrum and four lobes" by Pam Gregory, Tyler Junior College[3]

The Frontal Lobe is that portion of your brain that is directly behind your forehead and most often suffers injury due to its location. This area is responsible for solving problems, planning, generating emotions, controlling movements, and certain parts of your language and speech.

The Parietal Lobe is located directly behind the frontal lobe and near the top of the skull. This area is responsible for perceiving and processing outward information, such as when you touch something you understand it to be hot or cold, etc. This area works in conjunction with the Frontal Lobe to control movement, is responsible for recognition, and orientation.

The Temporal Lobe is located behind the Frontal Lobe and on the underside of the Parietal Lobe. This lobe works in conjunction with the Frontal Lobe to control language and speech. It is responsible for perceiving and processing everything you hear. This area is plays a key role in memory.

The Occipital Lobe is located behind both the Parietal and Temporal Lobes at the backside of your skull. It is the area responsible for vision and processing everything you see in your surroundings.

The next structure to be aware of is the Limbic System that plays a major role in the emotions we experience. As you can see in the following picture, this area of the brain is located deep inside the Cerebrum and is made up of several parts.

The Limbic System is the area of the brain that regulates emotion and memory. It directly connects the lower and higher brain functions. It influences emotions, the visceral responses to those emotions, motivation, mood, and sensations of pain and pleasure. The Limbic System is comprised of the following parts: Thalamus, Hypothalamus, Cingulate gyrus, Amygdala, Hippocampus, and Basal Ganglia.[6]

For purposes of our study here, two important parts of the limbic system to note are the hypothalamus and the amygdala. The hypothalamus controls emotional response, behavior, and sleep-wake cycles. The amygdala is a main control center for making associations from stimuli (information) and is thought to have a major role in self-voice recognition.

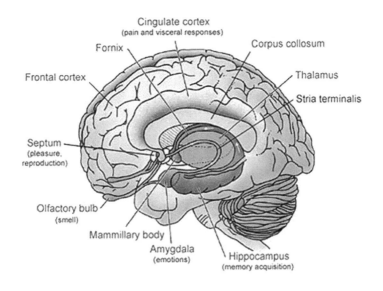

"Limbic System" by David Darling,[4]

There is new evidence to prove that the amygdala plays an important role for patients diagnosed with PTSD. A recent study conducted by scientists at Duke University in association with the Durham VA Medical Center (2012) found that people who suffered from PTSD had a smaller amygdala than others did. The study also noted, "Researchers found 20 years ago that there were changes in volume of the hippocampus associated with PTSD, but the amygdala is more relevant to the disorder."[7]

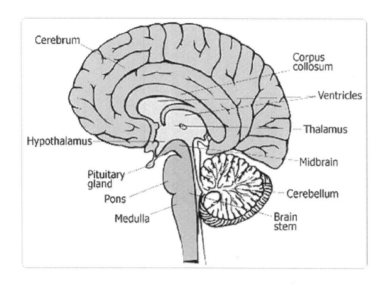

"Brain side view" © *American Medical Association.*
All Rights Reserved.[5]

The brainstem is the lower extension of the brain, located in front of the cerebellum and connected to the spinal cord. It consists of three structures the midbrain, the pons, and the medulla oblongata.

The brainstem serves as a relay station, passing messages back and forth between various paths of the body and the cerebral cortex. Many simple or primitive functions that are essential for survival are located here.

The midbrain is an important center for ocular motion while the pons is involved with coordinating eye and facial movements facial sensation, hearing and balance.

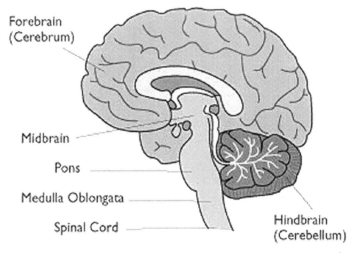

"Median coronal cross-section of the brain" by David Darling [6]

The medulla oblongata controls breathing, blood pressure, heart rhythms and swallowing. Messages from the cortex to the spinal cord and nerves that branch from the spinal cord are sent through the pons and the brainstem. Destruction of these regions of the brain causes "brain death." Without these keys functions, humans cannot survive. [7]

The next important topic of brain and body anatomy that we need to review is the Nervous System. This system is actually made of up of several parts.

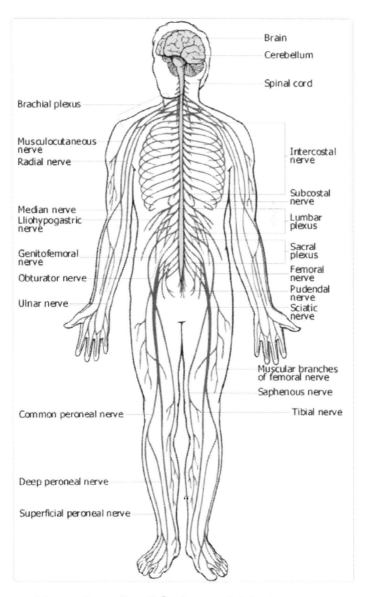

Labels:
Brain
Cerebellum
Spinal cord
Brachial plexus
Musculocutaneous nerve
Radial nerve
Intercostal nerve
Subcostal nerve
Median nerve
Lliohypogastric nerve
Lumbar plexus
Sacral plexus
Genitofemoral nerve
Femoral nerve
Obturator nerve
Pudendal nerve
Ulnar nerve
Sciatic nerve
Muscular branches of femoral nerve
Saphenous nerve
Common peroneal nerve
Tibial nerve
Deep peroneal nerve
Superficial peroneal nerve

Nervous System Basic" © American Medical Association.
All Rights Reserved.[7]

47

Your nervous system is composed of the central nervous system (CNS), the cranial nerves, and the peripheral nerves or peripheral nervous system (PNS).

The brain and spinal cord comprise your central nervous system. The network of nerves that connect at different levels of the spinal cord control both conscious and unconscious activities. It is through the spinal cord that information flows from these nerves to the brain and back again.[8]

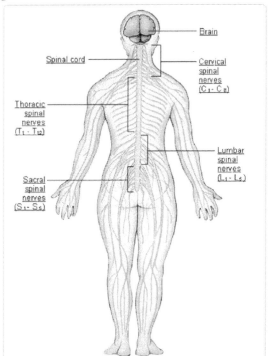

"Nervous System Groups of Nerves" © *American Medical Association. All Rights Reserved.*[8]

The cranial nerves connect the brain to the head. The four groups of nerves that branch from the cervical, thoracic, lumbar, and sacral regions of the spinal cord are called the peripheral nerves.[9]

Cells are the basic unit of the body. There are 210 types of cells in the body, but the cell related to this discussion is the Neuron. Neurons are nerve cells that are specific to the nervous system. Neurons differ from other cells in the body in that their primary function is to carry messages to all parts of the body.

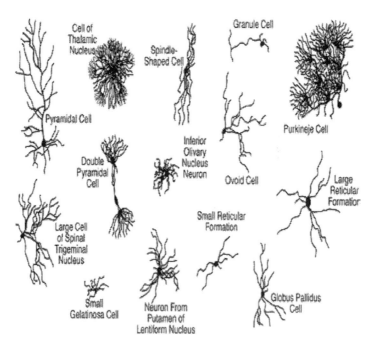

"Types of Neurons" by Dr. Robert Stufflebeam, CCSI [9]

The human brain has more than 100 billion neurons, with 14 to 16 billion in the cerebral cortex and nearly 100 billion in the cerebellum alone.[10]

Dr. Robert Stufflebeam of the Mind Project (2008) explains the actions of neurons in the brain as follows:

> Neurons are the basic information processing structures in the CNS. The function of a neuron is to receive INPUT "information" from other neurons, to process that information, then to send "information" as OUTPUT to other neurons. Synapses are connections between neurons through which "information" flows from one neuron to another. Hence, neurons process all of the "information" that flows within, to, or out of the CNS. All of it! All of the *motor* information through which we are able to move; all of the *sensory* information through which we are able to see, to hear, to smell, to taste, and to touch; and of course all of the *cognitive* information through which we are able to reason, to think, to dream, to plan, to remember, and to do everything else that we do with our minds.[11]

"Neuron On White Background" by jscreationzs / Free Digital Photos.net[10]

Neurons have three parts: Dendrites – receive information from another cell and transmit the message to the cell body, Cell body – contains the nucleus, mitochondria and other organelles typical of eukaryotic cells, and Axon – conducts messages away from the cell body.

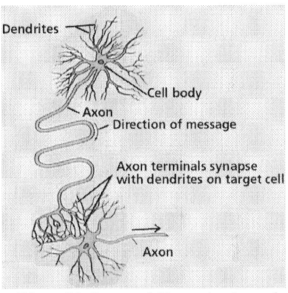

Dendrites

Cell body

Axon

Direction of message

Axon terminals synapse with dendrites on target cell

Axon

"Neurons" by Purves et al, Sinauer Associates and WH Freeman Publishers[11]

The junction between a nerve cell and another cell is called a synapse. Messages travel within the neuron as an electrical action potential. The space between two cells is known as the synaptic cleft. To cross the synaptic cleft requires the actions of neurotransmitters. Neurotransmitters are stored in small synaptic vesicles clustered at the tip of the axon.[12]

Neurotransmitters are chemicals released from the tip of an axon into the synaptic cleft when a nerve impulse arrives; neurotransmitters may stimulate or inhibit the next neuron.

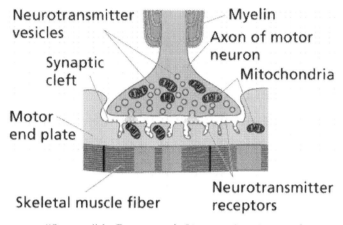

"Synapse" by Purves et al, Sinauer Associates and WH Freeman Publishers [12]

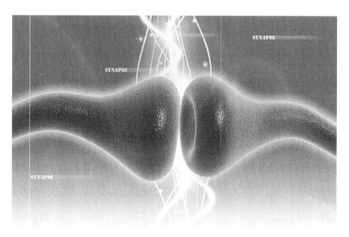

"Synapse" by Sheela Mohan / Free Digital Photos.net [13]

To explain this brain process another way, Dr. Carla Mathison (2007) at San Diego State University explains the brain's **Concept of Pruning**:

These neuronal pathways/bundles determine or shape our individual temperaments, talents, foibles and quirks as well as the quality of our thinking processes. The more synaptic firing that occurs across a specific connection, the stronger/denser the pathway becomes. The brain is very efficient. When the brain is 8 months old, it actually has twice as many neurons as the adult brain. As the brain ages, neurons that are weak or unused or simply don't fit the job that needs to be done are pruned away. This pruning leaves more efficient connections for those neurons that are performing the brain's work. The principle of 'Use it or lose it' begins, with non-working 'couch-potato' cells dying off while those that are exercised get stronger and develop more connections. At first, the neuronal activity that determines survival is random and spontaneous, but it becomes more organized as the fetus, and then the baby, receives input from its environment. Neurons that are heavily used form connections with other neurons. The process of neurons talking to one another is electro-chemical. The action within the neuron is electrical but the message becomes chemical as it travels between neurons. The chemicals traveling between neurons are called neurotransmitters. When two neurons come together, they don't actually touch. The dendrites of one neuron take information from the axon of another neuron through chemicals (neurotransmitters) flowing across what we call the SYNAPSE. Electricity fires the synapse and propels chemicals from the axon of one neuron to the dendrites of another, thus connecting the two neurons. [13]

You be familiar with neurotransmitters, especially Dopamine. The effect of Dopamine is what is referred to as the "runner's high" or what many athletes refer to as being "in the zone." As we exercise our bodies in a strenuous workout, run any great distance, or take a risk, our brain releases many endorphins to help us accomplish our task. The main neurotransmitter associated with this process is dopamine, which results in the feeling of euphoria or a natural high.

Some of the well-known neurotransmitters are Serotonin, Dopamine, Norepinephrine (Noradrenalin). The production of too much or too little of these chemicals in the brain can result in a variety of mental illnesses. In some cases, psychiatrists use medications to regulate the production of these neurotransmitters in order to stabilize mood and mental processes.

This is a basic overview of simple brain anatomy and function, but by now, you can begin see that the brain and its processes are extremely complicated. I hope that this section has sparked your interest in learning more. See the list in the back of the book entitled "Recommended Reading and Resources" for more information.

So what happens when we have a thought?

Physical and Emotional Reactions To Thoughts

Depending on the type of thought that occurs – from memory, from an outside source, or as a reaction to stimuli, etc. – numerous brain structures and parts become instantly activated. Think of a circuit board with hundreds of lights flickering on and off or think of a night sky on the 4th of July lit up by hundreds of fireworks. In less than a fraction of a second, the nerve cells – Neurons – carry messages to different parts of the body. As we learned in the preceding section, for the successful transfer of these messages to occur from one neuron to the next neuron, the neurotransmitters must best released in the proper amounts. When this process fails, we experience mood swings, instability, or a multitude of other symptoms.

Think of the way lights short circuit, usually they flicker for a moment and then go dark. In a way, the same thing can happen in our brains. When neurons are not firing properly and/or when not enough or too many neurotransmitters are released – it throws the body and mind into abnormal states. Consequently, these abnormal states result in mental and/or emotional illness, addictions, and/or an overall inability to live a quality life.

Keep in mind that there are numerous internal and external elements and/or influences that can affect a person's current thoughts and thinking patterns such as: diet, exercise, amount of sleep, environment, religious beliefs, etc. However, for simplicity, we are going to keep this discussion at a basic level of what occurs when we have a thought.

For example, in a well-adjusted normally emotionally healthy individual, a memory or thought might be triggered by a familiar smell in the air. This smell may remind the person of someone or something they once loved. The smell – a physical sensation - triggers the thought or memory. The thought or memory can then trigger a feeling of love or sadness. If a feeling of love occurs, a person may notice a warm fuzzy feeling in the pit of the stomach. If sadness is triggered, a hollow empty feeling in the pit of the stomach may occur. If the smell is associated with a past situation that was uncomfortable or difficult, the palms may become sweaty, breathing may become rapid or shallow. The well-adjusted normal person may dwell on specific details of the memory for a few seconds or minutes and then re-focus their mind on the present and let it go.

For a normal person in this type of experience, the smell in the air would have been perceived and interpreted by neurons in the frontal, parietal, and temporal lobes (remember the lights on the circuit board). Neurons become electrically charged and begin sending messages across the synapses and releasing neurotransmitters. Memories are triggered which activates more neurons, producing more messages carried through the nervous system to parts of the body, i.e. sweaty palms or twinge in the stomach, etc. This combined multitude of action and reaction can occur in fractions of a second. When the normal person refocuses their mind on the present, this entire process begins again with different parts of the brain and neurotransmitters released in order to return the mind to the present moment and regain focus and attention. The actual processes that occur in the brain and body in this type of experience are far more complex and take actual years of study to comprehend.

What happens in the individual that struggles to control their thoughts in the same situation? When a memory or thought is triggered, the mind essentially becomes stuck on the memory. In a similar way to a car stuck in the mud, the tire spins but the car never moves forward – the mind is stuck on the memory, replaying it repeatedly. As this replay continues over a period of time, a variety of emotional and bodily responses may occur such as sadness, tears, physical pain, loss of appetite, fatigue, loss of interest in activities, etc. Or at the other extreme - the replay may cause paranoia, hyper-vigilance, fear, anxiety, anger, rage, depression, etc.

As we learned in the previous example of what may occur in the normal person's brain, certain portions of the brain are stimulated (like the circuit board lighting up) while other sections of the brain seem to go into a non-active mode (like the light bulb going out). The difference in people with mental illness or addictions is that certain portions of the brain may become either overactive or underactive. Certain neurotransmitters and other chemicals may be released in too strong of a connection or too weak of a connection. As previously stated, the actual processes are extremely complex and too difficult to describe here, but this is a very simple and general idea of what can occur.

In the Response to Stress illustration, the effects of stress on three types of patients are compared, along with the differing levels of Cortisol and Corticotrophin as depicted by the thickness of the arrows. Cortisol is a steroid hormone that helps the body respond to stress. Corticotrophin actually drives the body's response to stress. As you can see in the diagram, they work in conjunction with each other. When you look at the diagram and compare the levels of Cortisol, you can see that as compared to a normal person, the Cortisol level in the person with Major Depression is decreased whereas in the patient with PTSD the Cortisol level is greatly increased. At the same time, in the patient with Major Depression the Corticotrophin is increased while the level in the patient with PTSD is greatly decreased.

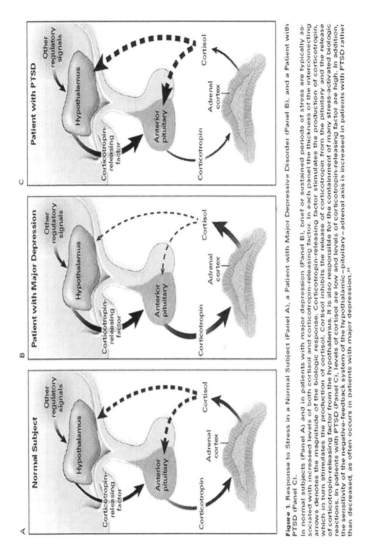

Figure 1. Response to Stress in a Normal Subject (Panel A), a Patient with Major Depressive Disorder (Panel B), and a Patient with PTSD (Panel C).

In normal subjects (Panel A) and in patients with major depression (Panel B), brief or sustained periods of stress are typically associated with increased levels of both cortisol and corticotropin-releasing factor. In each panel the thickness of the interconnecting arrows denotes the magnitude of the biologic response. Corticotropin-releasing factor stimulates the production of corticotropin, which in turn stimulates the production of cortisol. Cortisol inhibits the release of corticotropin from the pituitary and the release of corticotropin-releasing factor from the hypothalamus. It is also responsible for the containment of many stress-activated biologic reactions. In patients with PTSD (Panel C), levels of cortisol are low and levels of corticotropin-releasing factor are high. In addition, the sensitivity of the negative-feedback system of the hypothalamic–pituitary–adrenal axis is increased in patients with PTSD rather than decreased, as often occurs in patients with major depression.[1]

"Response to Stress" by Dr. Rachel Yehuda, Professor Psychiatry / Neuroscience, The Mount Sinai School of Medicine[1]

This type of opposite reaction is clearly seen in the behavior of these two patients during an experience when their symptoms are clear. The person with Major Depression loses their appetite, has no energy, and experiences a desire to sleep more. Whereas the person with PTSD, experiences irritability, anger, hypervigilence, agitation, and increased energy. This is a good example of the way that different levels of chemical processes in the brain can have an effect on thought, emotion, and behavior.

The person suffering major depression finds it difficult to be motivated to do anything and experiences a great deal of sadness. The person with PTSD constantly experiences events from the past, i.e. flashbacks and nightmares.

When we find a way to control our thoughts and/or our emotions, we have better control over our behavior and quality of life. There are two important concepts to understand here:

Thought ⟹ *Emotion* ⟹ *Action or Reaction*

Or

Emotion ⟹ *Thought* ⟹ *Action or Reaction*

Our thoughts can cause our emotions, which result in an action or reaction, or our emotions (feelings) can cause thoughts, which result in an action or reaction.

Think about what goes on in your mind and body as you are standing in line waiting to go on a ride like Space Mountain at Disneyland. You feel excitement and apprehension because your mind is telling you that you are going to enjoy this experience. You may feel restless and have a hard time standing still. Your thoughts may be that you wish the line would move along faster. You may notice a giddy feeling in your stomach like butterflies. By the time you actually sit down in your seat on the ride, you feel happy. Your thoughts about the ride created your emotions about the ride or your feelings of excitement created the thoughts that you are enjoying yourself.

Another common example is that if you listen to a sad love song that reminds you of a past relationship, one that you still have strong feelings about, notice what happens in your mind and body as you listen to the song. First, your mind goes back to the relationship. Your mind sees things you did together, precious and tender private moments you shared. Your mind may even hear loving words and secrets you shared. As you begin to re-experience this relationship in your mind, you notice a lump in your stomach or chest seeming to rise up to your throat. The lump turns into a deep aching sensation. Depending on the intensity of emotion connected with the relationship, you may start to feel an overwhelming sadness. Your breath becomes quicker and more labored and your eyes begin to release tears. Focus on your present surroundings fades. The longer you dwell on the song and replay the relationship in your mind, the more it physically hurts, and the more you cry.

If you dwell on negative situations long enough, you can lead yourself into a depression. A recent research study has identified the point when negative thoughts actually turn into clinical depression. Researchers Zauszniewski and Bekhet (2011) believe that large numbers of people can avoid developing mental illness if their negative thoughts can be identified and stopped in the beginning.[14]

One important aspect of creating and using a personal recording on a daily basis to train your brain to catch negative thinking patterns in the beginning and replace those thoughts with positive statements thereby changing the way your brain works and your mind thinks.

A study conducted by Zhu et al. (2012) found that the result of people with depression who repeatedly think about negative thoughts and memories, actually experience different patterns of brain network activation compared to healthy individuals.[15] The brain responds in either a healthy or an unhealthy way according to the thoughts you continually hold.

In a study conducted at the University of Manchester (2011) bipolar patients showed that their mood swings can be predicted, proof that talking therapies like cognitive behavioral therapy (CBT) can be an effective treatment. To date, the extreme swings of bipolar episodes have been attributed to a person's biological make-up. However, this study shows what a dramatic and important role thoughts and actions can play in controlling moods. For the patients who accepted their mood swings as a normal part of life and used tools to manage them, they faired through these episodes with less problems and less of an effect on their life. In contrast, patients who believed the mood swings were completely out of their control and that there was nothing they could do to change it, experienced more problems with a stronger effect on their lives.[16]

Just as we train babies to walk and talk with a great deal of effort over a period of time, it is possible to train our minds on how to respond to situations and challenges that arise as we go through our day in a positive healthy manner. This training process takes time, patience, and continuous focused effort.

Numerous neurologists and neuroscientists are now discovering that using positive thought (affirmations) on a regular basis actually produces physical structural changes in your brain through this retraining process.

Remember that we learned earlier in this chapter that the neurons in your brain communicate through the release of neurotransmitters and electrical energy across the synapse. Retraining your brain takes those synaptic connections and makes them stronger. By releasing neurotransmitters across the synaptic cleft to the same receptors over time, an actual learning process within the brain takes place.

For example, as people listen to themselves speaking a positive statement or repeatedly thinking a positive thought, the neurotransmitter Serotonin is released from the axon of the neuron across the synaptic cleft to the neurotransmitter receptors on the other side of the synapse. The neurotransmitter receptors actually gobble up the Serotonin. As this process is repeated with neurons firing in the same sequence, after so many times it becomes an automatic process. A stronger connection or bond is formed across the synapse and creates a connection memory resulting in a learning process having taken place.

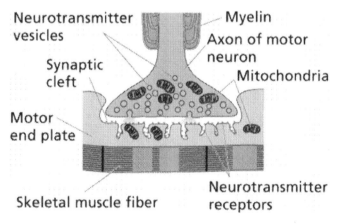

"Synapse" by Purves et al, Sinauer Associates and WH Freeman Publishers [12]

This is the whole point of making a personalized recording with your positive affirmations, in your own voice and listening to it every day and every night. This is what it accomplishes in your brain. It makes stronger connections between the synapses and creates a stronger bond to automatically remember those connections.

This is the process we are going to use to get your brain on a new track. To get your mind unstuck from the mud and keep your tires from spinning and going nowhere.

When you create your personalized recording according to the instructions outlined in Chapter 4, you are training your brain to respond to life in a healthy and positive way. You are creating stronger neural connections. You are fully utilizing the correct way in which God intended our brains to work to enrich your life and be a blessing to everyone around you.

Chapter 2 - References

1. Chudler, E. (n.d.). *Milestones in Neuroscience Research.* Washington University, History of Neuroscience, Faculty pages.
http://faculty.washington.edu/chudler/hist.html

2. Searle, J.R. (1992). "The Problem of Consciousness." University of Massachusettes Boston, Philosophy Department.
http://www.faculty.umb.edu/adam_beresford/courses/phil_100_11/reading_problem_of_consciousness.pdf

3. Merriam-Webster Dictionary Online (2012). Merriam-Webster, Inc. Encyclopedia Britannica Company.
http://www.merriam-webster.com/dictionary/consciousness?show=0&t=1352050821

4. Merriam-Webster Dictionary Online (2012). Merriam-Webster, Inc. Encyclopedia Britannica Company.
http://www.merriam-webster.com/dictionary/unconsciousness

5. *Corpus Collosum* (n.d.) Macalester College, Psychology, Corpus Callosum Web site.
http://www.macalester.edu/psychology/whathap/ubnrp/split_brain/Corpus%20Callosum.html

6. Mathison, Carla (2007). "Intro to the Brain." San Diego State University, Instructional Technology Services, Multimedia, Mathison.
http://its.sdsu.edu/multimedia/mathison/limbic/index.htm

7. Duke University Medical Center (2012), November 5). PTSD linked to smaller brain area regulating fear response. *Science Daily.* http://www.sciencedaily.com/releases/2012/11/12110516 1355.htm

8. American Medical Association (2012). Resources, Patient Education Materials, Atlas of the Human Body, Nervous System – Basic. http://www.ama-assn.org/ama/pub/physician-resources/patient-education-materials/atlas-of-human-body/nervous-system-basic.page

9. American Medical Association (2012). Resources, Patient Education Materials, Atlas of the Human Body, Nervous System – Groups of Nerves. http://www.ama-assn.org/ama/pub/physician-resources/patient-education-materials/atlas-of-human-body/nervous-system-groups.page

10. Burt, A.M. (1993). "Organization and Development of the Nervous System," "Brain Stem and Cerebellum," "Telencephalon," and "Cerebral Cortex." In *Textbook of Neuroanatomy.* Philadelphia, PA: W. B. Saunders, Co., 1993. Brain, Biology Encyclopedia. http://www.biologyreference.com/Bl-Ce/Brain.html

11. Stufflebeam, Robert (2008). "Neurons, Synapses, Action Potentials, and Neurotransmission." Consortium on Cognitive Science Instruction (CCSI), The Mind Project, Illinois State University. http://www.mind.ilstu.edu/curriculum/neurons_intro/neurons_intro.php

12. Farabee, Mike J. (2007). "The Nervous System: The Neuron." Estrella Mountain Community College, Biology Book.
http://www.emc.maricopa.edu/faculty/farabee/BIOBK/BioBookNERV.html

13. Mathison, Carla (2007). "Intro to the Brain." San Diego State University, Instructional Technology Services, Multimedia, Mathison.
http://its.sdsu.edu/multimedia/mathison/neuron/index.htm

14. Zauszniewski, J.A.& A.K. Bekhet. "Screening Measure for Early Detection of Depressive Symptoms: The Depressive Cognition Scale." *Western Journal of Nursing Research*, 2011:34 (2):230 DOI: 10.1177/0193945910396731, January 31, 2011.

15. Xueling Zhu, Xiang Wang, Jin Xiao, Jian Liao, Mingtian Zhong, Wei Wang, Shuqiao Yao. (2012). "Evidence of a Dissociation Pattern in Resting-State Default Mode Network Connectivity in First-Episode, Treatment-Naïve Major Depression Patients." *Biological Psychiatry*, 2012; 71 (7): 611 DOI: 10.1016/j.biopsych.2011.10.035

16. University of Manchester (2011). Mood swings of bipolar patients can be predicted, study shows. *Science Daily*.
http://www.sciencedaily.com/releases/2011/04/110418201739.htm

Illustrations:

1. Neuron by Dream Designs / Free Digital Photos.net
   http://www.freedigitalphotos.net/images/Human_body_g
   281-Neuron_p65093.html

2. Cerebral Hemispheres by Pam Gregory, Professor of
   Biology, Biology Department, Tyler Junior College.
   http://science.tjc.edu/images/brain/Index.htm

3. Cerebrum and four lobes by Pam Gregory, Professor of
   Biology, Biology Department, Tyler Junior College.
   http://science.tjc.edu/images/brain/Index.htm

4. Limbic System by David Darling, The Encyclopedia of
   Science, Limbic System.
   http://www.daviddarling.info/encyclopedia/L/limbic_syste
   m.html

5. Brain side view by © American Medical Association.
   All Rights Reserved.
   http://www.ama-assn.org/ama/pub/physician-
   resources/patient-education-materials/atlas-of-human-
   body/brain-side-view.page?

6. Median coronal cross-section of the brain by David Darling,
   The Encyclopedia of Science, Brainstem.
   http://www.daviddarling.info/encyclopedia/B/brainstem.h
   tml

7. Nervous System Basic by © American Medical Association.
   All Rights Reserved.
   http://www.ama-assn.org/ama/pub/physician-
   resources/patient-education-materials/atlas-of-human-
   body/nervous-system-basic.page?

8. Nervous System – Groups of Nerves by © American

Medical Association. All Rights Reserved.
http://www.ama-assn.org/ama/pub/physician-
resources/patient-education-materials/atlas-of-human-
body/nervous-system-groups.page

9. Types of Neurons by Dr. Robert Stufflebeam, Consortium
on Cognitive Science Instruction (CCSI), The Mind Project,
Illinois State University.
http://www.mind.ilstu.edu/curriculum/neurons_intro/neu
rons_intro.php

10. Neuron On White Background by jscreationzs / Free
Digital Photos.net
http://www.freedigitalphotos.net/images/Human_body_g
281-Neuron_On_White_Background_p15761.html

11. Neurons by Purves et al., Life: The Science of Biology, 4th
Edition, by Sinauer Associates and WH Freeman
publishers.
http://www.emc.maricopa.edu/faculty/farabee/biobk/Bio
BookNERV.html

12. Synapse by Purves et al., Life: The Science of Biology, 4th
Edition, by Sinauer Associates and WH Freeman
publishers.
http://www.emc.maricopa.edu/faculty/farabee/biobk/Bio
BookNERV.html

13. Synapse by Sheela Mohan / Free Digital Photos.net
http://www.freedigitalphotos.net/images/Human_body_g
281-Synapse_p82919.html

14. Response to Stress by Dr. Rachel Yehuda, Professor
Psychiatry / Neuroscience, The Mount Sinai School of
Medicine[12]

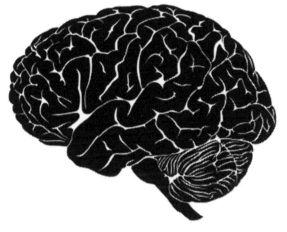

Human Brain by smokedsalmon / Free Digital Photos.net

"… their minds became dark and confused."

Romans 1:21 (NLT)

A GOOD BRAIN WASHING

Chapter 3:
Brainwashing History

To begin our discussion in this chapter, I need to make clear that the purpose of this book and workbook is not to give anyone or anything control over your mind. The main goal of everything presented within these pages, is for you and God to take control over your own mind and behavior.

First, you need to become aware of your own individual thinking patterns, the statements you believe about yourself, and the statements others make to you or about you, that you choose to believe. Secondly, you need to see how these thinking patterns and thoughts affect your behavior and your life. Finally, this material is presented to provide you with a realistic and practical tool to change your thinking and your behavior.

By making positive changes in your thinking and behavior, you are able to achieve your goals and dreams, enjoy peace of mind, and mental/emotional stability. You might be saying, "Yeah right, I've heard all of this before!" Okay, I am willing to concede that you have probably heard similar promises from other sources, but you have never heard them in relation to the use of a personalized recording that directly changes your brain and you have never heard them from me. I have successfully used the tool outlined in this book for the past decade and seen dramatic changes in my thoughts and behavior, as well as watching my faith grow rapidly. I have seen the impossible become possible.

To be clear, as opposed to brainwashing – in this book we are "washing out our brains" to get rid of the negatives or more simply, retraining the mind and remapping the brain with positive influences. However, so you can understand the extreme difference, I have included a brief history of brainwashing.

When most people first hear the word brainwashing, they immediately associate the term with something dark. Images come to mind of a cult with zombie like characters or hundreds of mindless people with blank stares wandering around. Both of those ideas are not far from the truth. Usually the first groups we might think of are the Manson Family, the followers of David Koresh in Waco, or Jonestown. It is certainly reasonable to assume those people were brainwashed. Their actions and behaviors were far from what we consider normal in our society. There are some excellent books on brainwashing by scholars far more knowledgeable than I am on this subject. I have included their books in the list of recommended reading for those of you who would like to explore this topic in further detail.

History of Brainwashing

In its most basic form, brainwashing is described as a person or group taking control over another person's thought and behavior in order to conform to the leader or group's expectations. Usually the term brainwashing is reserved for the most extreme cases and involves some form of torture or deprivation of basic survival needs.

There are degrees of mind control that vary from group to group or situation to situation. Looking at a scale and proceeding from weak to strong in the levels of mind control, we can look at the following words and their definitions and then discuss each one briefly. Merriam-Webster (2012) defines the following words as:

Influence:[1]

the act or power of producing an effect without apparent exertion of force or direct exercise of command; the power or capacity of causing an effect in indirect or intangible ways

Suggest:[2]

to seek to influence; to mention or imply as a possibility; to propose as desirable or fitting; to offer for consideration or as a hypothesis; *suggestion* - the process by which a physical or mental state is influenced by a thought or idea

Persuade:[3]
to move by argument, entreaty, or expostulation [discussion or examination] to a belief, position, or course of action

Manipulate:[4]
to manage or utilize skillfully; to control or play upon by artful, unfair, or insidious means especially to one's own advantage

Coerce:[5]
to restrain or dominate by force; to compel to an act or choice; to achieve by force or threat

Brainwash:[6]
a forcible indoctrination to induce someone to give up basic political, social, or religious beliefs and attitudes and to accept contrasting regimented ideas

Brainwashing:[7]

Concise Encyclopedia's explanation:

Systematic effort to destroy an individual's former loyalties and beliefs and to substitute loyalty to a new ideology or power. It has been used by religious CULTS as well as by radical political groups. The techniques of brainwashing usually involve isolation from former associates and sources of information; an exacting regimen calling for absolute obedience and humility; strong social pressures and rewards for cooperation; physical and psychological punishments for noncooperation, including social ostracism and criticism, deprivation of food, sleep, and social contacts, bondage, and torture; and constant reinforcement. Its effects are sometimes reversed through deprogramming, which combines confrontation and intensive psychotherapy.

We all experience a variety of 'influences' as we grow from babies to children to adults. The first people to exhibit a strong influence in our lives are our parents. We learn boundaries and limitations by what we are allowed to do and not do. Some Native American cultures teach their children by experience when they will not listen to reason. My father related an example from our ancestors, an adult tells a child not to stick their hand in the fire several times, but the child may be stubborn in nature and keeps testing the boundary. The adult then lets the child experience a slight burn on the fingertips. The pain created by the burning sensation is enough to teach the child a valuable lesson that the child remembers for the rest of their life – respect for fire and the potential danger of getting too close to a fire. The father allowed the natural consequence to influence ongoing safe behavior in the child.

As we progress through our school years, we learn

the meaning of 'suggestion' from various authority figures. How many times have we heard the phrase, "I suggest you …" when talking about studying to make good grades, practicing our music or sports ability on a daily basis, rehearsing songs or lines for a play, etc. Parents often say, "I strongly suggest you …" in relation to boundaries or discipline. We learn very quickly that if we want to keep from losing our privileges and freedoms we had better listen to their guidance and cooperate.

As we discussed in chapter 1, our childhood environments, peers, and media use powers of influence, suggestion, and persuasion to bring us around to their way of thinking.

When we enter adulthood and become a part of the regular working population. We encounter another set of influences and suggestions that define our behavior and thinking. In order to keep our job or excel in our chosen career, we must adhere to the normal expected behaviors of our environment. If someone works in an office with clients, professional business dress is expected. Certain standards apply to conversation and are common among employees. You would not hear the same loud expressions you may hear in a nightclub, in a professional office environment.

Similarly, if you join a branch of law enforcement or a branch of the military, you must attend either a training academy or boot camp. The purpose of these learning environments is to insure that each person acts and reacts according to a standard that has been researched and refined to ensure safety for all members and a successful mission. Realistically, how good would a police force be at protection if they only enforced the law when they felt like it? We would not have a very safe society to live in if that were the case. How well would a combat unit be able to perform and accomplish their mission if each member did their own thing? Therefore, we can see that some influences, suggestions, or persuasions are necessary for the normal standard of our society to function successfully.

The line towards brainwashing is crossed when it comes to any type of harm or unhealthy control forced upon another person. Take for example the case of domestic violence. The abuser may be insecure, possessive, or overly jealous of their partner. First, they begin by cutting off all outside associations with family members and friends, thereby isolating their partner into a total dependence on them. In this way, the abuser can exert total control over their partner and manipulate every aspect of their behavior. Most of the time they brainwash their partner into believing that without the abuser, the victim cannot survive or convince the victim that no one else would want them. Since it is impossible to please anyone all of the time and since most of these abusers resort to violence, the victim often suffers harshly and more frequently as time goes on. Some abusers may sincerely apologize after a violent episode, even have tears in their eyes and offer flowers with a promise that it will never happen again. They may be very sincere in their expressions of regret. Sadly, it does happen repeatedly and gets worse over time. The only way to end this abusive cycle is to get away from the abuser permanently.

A CIA psychological warfare specialist acting undercover as a journalist, named Edward Hunter in 1950, first introduced the actual word "brainwashing". Hunter wrote an article for the Miami Daily News, entitled "Brain-Washing Tactics Force Chinese into Ranks of Communist Party." Hunter continued to produce numerous articles and books on the subject. The origins of Hunter's articles were based on the experiences of American soldiers who were captured during the Korean War and brutally tortured by Chinese Communists. Some of the American prisoners were brainwashed into embracing communism as the only true path to follow in life. They were starved, beaten, forced to go without sleep, and subjected to extreme emotional and mental duress. They were relentlessly pushed with excruciating mental, physical, and emotional pain beyond all humane treatment until they were broken down into a hollow reflection of the person that existed before capture. The extent of their experience was so severe that many of them still had not fully recovered years after their release. Today we know that most of them if not all, were suffering from PTSD or Post Traumatic Stress Syndrome.

Even though this familiar word "brainwashing" was

not used until 1950 in the English language, the same concept and practices were used in varying degrees far back into early history. In the 1550 B.C., brainwashing techniques are described in the Egyptian Book of the Dead. These techniques, based on trauma to the body and mind, were the basis for what was previously known as the Russian KGB method. These methods were also adapted by the secret sect, the Illuminati which was founded in 1776.[8] You may remember the Illuminati from Dan Brown's book and subsequent film with Tom Hanks by the same name, *The Da Vinci Code*.[9] Other groups known to have used these methods include secret societies, religious cults, and German Nazis.

In the 20th century, brainwashing or mind control was not only used by the Chinese Communists, but also by the Russians in the old USSR in prison camps referred to as the GULAG (Glavnoe Upravlenie Ispravitel-no-trudovykh Lagerei). The Gulag was "run by Soviet KGB agents in the 1930'-60s, the largest world's laboratory for mind control experiments with over 10,000,000 'guinea pigs' [people] sacrificed."[8]

Aside from a few rumors, most of the U.S. population was not aware that this was taking place in Russia. Similarly, most Americans had no idea of the horrendous nature or cruel and tortuous extent of the experiments that were being conducted by Dr. Mengele on Jewish prisoners at the concentration camps in Auschwitz during World War II. Hitler gave Dr. Mengele aka The Angel of Death, free reign to do whatever he wanted to both children and adults. Both men are considered pure evil in human flesh by many people around the world. Dr. Mengele's experiments constituted the basis for ongoing mind control research conducted by the CIA in the program MK-ULTRA and the Monarch Method. These techniques are based on sadism and often result in producing a person with Multiple Personality Disorder (MPD) or more currently known as Dissociative Identity Disorder (DID) in order to be effectively controlled by a "handler."[8]

Robert Condon, explored this type of control in the book "The Manchurian Candidate" first published in 1959. John Frankenheimer made the book into a feature length film in 1962 starring Frank Sinatra, Laurence Harvey, Angela Lansberry, James Gregory, and Henry Silva.[10] A modern version of the film set during the Persian Gulf War was released in 2004 and produced by Frank Sinatra's daughter Tina, along with Scott Rudin and Johnan Demme. Demme also directed a cast that included Denzel Washington, Liev Schreiber, Meryl Streep, Jon Voight, Jeffrey Wright, and Kimberly Elise, along with many talented others.[11] In both films; a unit of soldiers are kidnapped and brainwashed. The earlier film portrays a collection of Foreign Communists as the enemy conducting the brainwashing with one soldier as the controlled killer. The modern version portrays a U.S. company and government contractor as the enemy conducting the brainwashing with two soldiers forced to kill. If you want to get a good visual understanding of the effects of brainwashing and the damage it can do, you should read the book and watch both of these films. Additionally, you can find testimonies of people who have experienced brainwashing on the internet. Years later, they are still devastated and struggling to live a somewhat normal life.

Most of the people in America are aware of the reference to brainwashing in relation to the Tate-LaBianca murders committed by the Manson Family in 1969.[12] People couldn't help but wonder how Manson had brainwashed these young adults into committing such heinous and horrible acts of murder with no provocation on the part of the victims. Manson was an expert at finding a person's weaknesses and using those as a basis of manipulation in order to carrying out his insane horrendous and violent fantasies against innocent victims.

The concept of brainwashing was brought to public view again during trial of Patty Hearst in 1975. Patty was the granddaughter of the famous William Randolph Hearst, who had made millions from his media investments. Patty was kidnapped by the Symbionese Liberation Army (SLA) and tortured during her captivity. She was repeatedly raped by multiple members of the SLA, forced to spend days on end in a dark closet, and physically beaten numerous times. Months later she participated in a several robberies with her captives, was arrested, and sent to prison.[13]

Unfortunately, the jury failed to comprehend the extent of her brainwashing. If you look at the facts that this young girl was raised in a plush, clean, and protected environment. Her daily life probably included maids, a personal attendant, a loving – nurturing family, and all the luxuries she wanted. Then, suddenly, she is shoved into a dark space, starved, cold, raped, beaten, and forced to be with vulgar people who probably stunk from not bathing regularly. The immediate drastic change in her surroundings coupled with the violence and abuse she was forced to endure, broke her down mentally, emotionally, and physically. In order to survive, she became a part of her environment. The fear of the unknown coupled with the fear of death – especially a long and painful one for a frightened child (in my opinion she was probably still a child emotionally), must have been the most horrible thing she could experience.

This same breaking point that many victims reach is the victory point for the person or group inflicting the brainwashing. It is the moment that they gain total control over their victim's mind and body. Thus creating a puppet in human form to do whatever evil bidding they program the person to do. The person that existed before the brainwashing, is dead and gone, never to return. The connections in the brain that made this person who they were before suffering at the hands of their captives, have been broken beyond repair. Their former sense of self usually never returns. Even after years of therapy, some victims still suffer tremendously with horrible nightmares, flashbacks, and numerous physical symptoms.

There are more subtle forms of brainwashing that are less violent, at least in the beginning. There are the familiar religious cults such as David Koresh's group in Waco, and Jonestown in Guyana. In the beginning, these groups prey on individuals that are lacking something in their lives and searching for answers. These victims feel empty and unfulfilled. A certain leader or group convinces these people that they have the only "true" answer. Very slowly, over time, people are indoctrinated into the group by subtle persuasions. Eventually they are convinced that the group is the most important thing in their life and the only way to happiness or to enjoy eternity. The group leader or leaders reinforce the belief that they are the only person(s) that know the truth. These groups begin crossing the line into dangerous territory when, as in the case of domestic violence, they start cutting people off from their families and friends, taking control of their money and assets, and leading them into isolation with the members of the group as their only peers.

What begins as an innocent spiritual journey often ends in tragedy. Usually the leaders are mentally ill in some capacity and almost always suffer from some degree of paranoia. Once they have assembled a large enough group, they move their group to an isolated area such as the compound in Waco or the plantation in Guyana. Intervention on the part of families and friends becomes difficult. Even an attempted escape by members of the group becomes a difficult proposition.

As the mental and/or physical illness of the leader declines and the conflict with the outside world escalates, the only resolution becomes destruction and devastation. In the case of Koresh's group in Waco, the ATF (Bureau of Alcohol, Tobacco, and Firearms) attempted to serve a search warrant. When that resulted in a two-hour gun battle with 4 agents and 6 members killed, the FBI (Federal Bureau of Investigation) intervened and a siege ensued lasting 50 days, ending with a fire devastating the compound. The result was that 76 men, women, and children died in the fire along with David Koresh.[14]

In the case of Jonestown located in Guyana, Brazil, often referred to as the Jonestown massacre, 918 American people died, which included 200 murdered children. Also included was U.S. Representative Leo Ryan who had led a group of media and concerned relatives to Jonestown to conduct an investigation. From the Jonestown population, 15 members were shot and killed on a plane while attempting to leave and return to the United States. It is estimated that there were over 1100 people at Jonestown at the time of the massacre. Some are believed to have escaped into the surrounding jungle and some survivors were airlifted to a U.S. Air Force evacuation aircraft in Georgetown.[15]

How could Jim Jones have convinced so many

hundreds of people to commit mass suicide and murder their children? The answer is brainwashing, conducted slowly and methodically over a long period of time. He convinced his followers that the outside world was the enemy. He convinced them that if they did not obey him, they, along with their children would be brutally attacked and murdered by people from outside of their group.

There are some groups who use much subtler techniques and do not end in violence, but may be just as dangerous when it comes to individual identity. For example, the "Moonies" is a term that was applied to the followers of Reverend Moon of the Unification Church in the 1970s.

I remember a trip to Washington, D.C. with my parents. As we were touring the city, there were a large number of people standing on corners and handing out flyers and wearing white jump suits with a sash that read 'God Bless America'. As one of the young men approached me to hand me a flyer, I was surprised by his eyes. Although he smiled at me, his eyes were empty, zombie like with his pupils too dilated for a sunny day. It made a chill run down my spine. The flyer was about Reverend Moon and the Unification Church.

Steve Hassan, a former member who became one of the cult leaders after only 3 months of membership relates that upon joining he was "…told to drop out of school, donate my bank account, look at Moon as my true parent, and believe my parents were Satan." It took a vehicle crash and his family's intervention with deprogramming to return him to a somewhat normal state of mind.[16]

How this book is NOT Brainwashing

This book is not brainwashing in any sense of the word. Neither is it the basis for allowing anyone or anything to have control over your mind and subsequently your life. As we have seen in the previous examples, one of the first signs of danger is any person or group that wants to separate you from your family, friends, money, or assets. If you encounter any individual or group that attempts to do that to you in any way whatsoever – RUN – run away from them as far and as fast as you can. No matter how slick, subtle, or soothing their message may be – it is very dangerous to you and your future.

First, as we have seen in the definition and the preceding examples, brainwashing involves separating an individual from their family and friends. This book does not do that in any way whatsoever. In fact, the use of this tool encourages healthy relationships with family and friends and encourages focusing on the positive aspects of those around you. It focuses on loving people unconditionally without expectations.

Second, as noted in the introduction and the author's note in the beginning of the book, this tool does not have all of the answers to anyone's problems. Rather, it is an effective method to aid support systems already in place in an individual's life or to point someone in the right direction.

Third, there is no cult or group leader being presented here. Each person is directed to form their own intimate relationship with God and allow Him to direct their thinking, goals, and aspirations.

Finally, there is no deprivation or suffering as a result of the principles presented in this book. The use of the tool presented is to promote a healthy and whole life. To motivate and inspire readers to persist in reaching toward spiritual, mental, and emotional growth and balance.

This book is a tool to renew your mind and explore your individuality. A way for you and God to take control of your mind and train your brain to respond to life in a healthy and whole manner using the wisdom and intelligence that God has placed within each one of us. This tool is an effective aid to helping you to grow spiritually, mentally, and emotionally.

Chapter 3 - References

1.-7. Merriam-Webster Dictionary Online (2012).
Merriam-Webster, Inc. Encyclopedia Britannica
Company.

1. http://www.merriam-webster.com/dictionary/influence
2. http://www.merriam-webster.com/dictionary/suggest?show=0&t=1352246845
3. http://www.merriam-webster.com/dictionary/persuade
4. http://www.merriam-webster.com/dictionary/manipulate?show=0&t=1352247292
5. http://www.merriam-webster.com/dictionary/coerce
6. http://www.merriam-webster.com/dictionary/brainwash
7. http://www.merriam-webster.com/dictionary/brainwash

8. Rakhimov, A. (2012). "Brainwashing Techniques: KGB
vs. CIA." http://www.normalbreathing.com/brainwashing-techniques.php#.UH9mRW8d_Tr

9. Howard, R. et al. (Producer) and Howard, R.
(Director). (2006). The Da Vinci Code [Motion
Picture]. United States: Columbia Pictures/Imagine
Entertainment.
http://www.imdb.com/title/tt0382625/

10. Frankenheimer, J. et al. (Producer) and
Frankenheimer, J. (Director). (1962). The Manchurian
Candidate [Motion Picture]. United States: M.C.
Productions/United Artists.
http://www.imdb.com/title/tt0056218/

11. Sinatra, T. et al. (Producers) and Demme, J. (Director). (2004). The Manchurian Candidate [Motion Picture]. United States: Paramount Pictures. http://www.imdb.com/title/tt0368008/

12. Linder, D. (2002). "The Charles Manson (Tate-LaBianca Murder) Trial." University of Missouri-Kansas City, Law Department, Faculty Projects. http://law2.umkc.edu/faculty/projects/ftrials/manson/mansonaccount.html

13. Taylor, K. (2004). *Brainwashing: The Science of thought control.* New York: Oxford University Press. pg. 10.

14. Ramsland, K. (n.d.). "David Koresh: Millennial Violence, David Korech and the Waco Incident: Both Side Prepare." Crime Library, Criminal Minds and Methods. http://www.trutv.com/library/crime/notorious_murders/not_guilty/koresh/1.html

15. Steel, F. (n.d.). "Jonestown Massacre: A'Reason' to Die." Crime Library, Criminal Minds and Methods. http://www.trutv.com/library/crime/notorious_murders/mass/jonestown/index_1.html

16. Saner, E (2012). "Interview with Steve Hassan: Moonie Cult Leader." The Guardian, UK. http://www.guardian.co.uk/world/2012/sep/03/moonie-cult-leader

Illustrations

1. Human Brain by smokedsalmon / Free Digital Photos.net
http://www.freedigitalphotos.net/images/Human_body_g281-Human_Brain_p34113.html

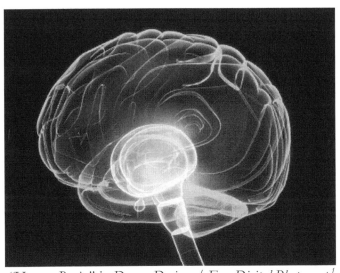

"Human Brain" by Dream Designs / Free Digital Photos.net [1]

"For God hath not given us the spirit of fear; but of power, and of love, and of a sound mind."

2 Timothy 1:7 (KJV)

Chapter 4:
DO'S AND DON'TS IN A PERSONAL RECORDING

Our focus is to replace negative and destructive thinking with positive thinking. As a result, we are replacing poor choices with wise choices, along with replacing destructive behavior with healthy behavior. The goal is to attain stability, clarity, and a stronger mental focus.

Using Your Own Voice

There are specific reasons why hearing your own voice on a recording is much more powerful than listening to someone else's voice. First, in the same way we learned that a fetus in the womb recognizes sounds like a mother's voice; your brain recognizes your own voice. You can compare it to a room full of new recruits in a boot camp barracks. They are sitting around talking in a noisy group, but as soon as the Drill Sergeant appears and someone yells "ATTENTION", everyone stops

95

talking, immediately stands up at the 'Attention' position, giving the Drill Sergeant their full focus and concentration. In a way, the same thing happens in your brain when you speak to yourself. All other thoughts fade and your brain immediately focuses its attention on your voice.

Neuroscientists refer this to as self-recognition or self-voice recognition. In a study at Oxford University, Kaplan et al. (2008) reported increased brain activity, specifically in the right hemisphere of the brain, in the inferior frontal gyrus as a direct result of listening to one's own voice.[1]

Remember the lighted circuit board idea from Chapter 2? When you speak aloud, the right side of your brain becomes highly active (all the lights go on). Your brain recognizes its own voice and we now have the science to prove it. There are numerous meditation recordings available on a variety of topics and I am not discounting their ability to help anyone. However, it comes down to a matter of the degree of power. If your car became stuck in deep mud on an isolated road, would you rather have a little car trying to pull you out or a big truck? If you want to experience the strongest possible results, you need to have the big truck.

This is one reason why is it so important to pay attention to what we are telling ourselves. Our brains are listening and ready to carry out our commands.

We need to pay attention to our thoughts!

If we constantly tell ourselves what a bad person we are, then our brains make decisions and take actions to prove that we are a bad person.

My favorite dessert is a bowl of French vanilla ice cream with a large scoop of peanut butter, topped with chocolate syrup. When I focus my thoughts on that dessert and how much I enjoy it, within a short time I am figuring out a way to get that dessert.

Try it for yourself right now. Think about your favorite candy bar or dessert. Think about the rich color, the enticing smell, how it would look on a plate in front of you at this moment. Think about how good it tastes when you take that first bite. See yourself taking a fork or a spoon and getting a big piece. Think about the flavor slowly melting into your mouth. Think about how it feels on your tongue and how delicious and satisfying it is as it slides down your throat. Notice what is starting to happen after a few minutes of focusing on this example. Your mouth may be beginning to water, your stomach may be starting to turn and growl. Pretty soon, your mind is figuring out a way to get that dessert, so you can put it in your mouth and satisfy the desire your brain created in your body.

One of the benefits to using this recording on a daily basis is that you are training your mind to catch negative thoughts and replace them with positive thoughts, before your brain has a chance to dwell on the negative and carry out negative action.

The well-known Bible teacher and author Joyce Meyer states:

> Our words are not forced on us; they formulate in our thoughts and then we speak them. We can learn to choose our thoughts, to resist wrong ones and think on good, healthy, and right ones. Where the mind goes, the man follows. We could also say, where the mind goes, the mouth follows! [2]

Joyce is not referring to eating in this example, but to the way the words we speak produce an effect in our lives. She is also making a very important point here about the ability we have in making choices regarding our thoughts.

As noted in the workbook section, some of the affirmation examples include replacing specific thinking. Here are two examples from my personal recording:

"When faced with a problem or crisis, I respond with calmness and wisdom"

"When faced with a problem or challenge, my mind immediately focuses on solutions"

This may sound like it is too easy, but I am here to tell you it works. As I have previously stated, I have been using this recording for the past ten years, and I have seen dramatic changes in my mind and behavior. Where once I would react in anger or depression, I now focus on the solutions to a problem.

Here is a specific example from my past. If a friend said, she would call me on a certain day and then did not call. I would immediately assume that she did not care about our friendship or me. I would get angry or hurt or both. My mind would tell me that she had other friends who were more important to her and that she was probably spending time with them. I would get myself so upset that by the time I saw her again, I would say something mean or sarcastic and ruin our friendship. Today, if a friend does not call when she said she would, my mind thinks of possible interferences. Such as she had a crisis of her own to handle, or one of her children were having a problem, or she was distracted with too many things and simply forgot. In any of the scenarios, there is no reason to get upset. I have trained my mind to get off a self-serving, self-centered track, and to think more along the lines of concern for her than for myself. I have trained my mind to love unconditionally. As a result of this type of brain training, I feel more confident in my relationships, and experience a higher quality of relationship with the people in my life.

Another example occurred more recently. My garbage disposal stopped working several days before I was having people over for dinner. In the past, I would have freaked out because when playing hostess, everything in my house had to be absolutely perfect. What I would have done before, would be to go borrow money to buy a new garbage disposal, and pay extra for a handyman to rush over and install it. Then, I would have had to struggle on the next payday to figure out how to pay the bills and pay back the money I borrowed. Instead, because I have trained my mind to respond with calmness and wisdom, and to look for solutions, I decided to do things the old-fashioned way. I cleaned out the side of the sink with the garbage disposal by hand. I put the old food scraps in a bag, tied it up, and put it in the garbage can. Problem solved. Amazing! No one at the dinner party even noticed that my garbage disposal did not work. I was able to enjoy my guests without freaking out and without putting a strain on my finances.

When we train our minds to think and respond the way God intended when he created our wonderful brains, we enjoy a fuller and happier life in every area of our lives.

Avoid Negative Statements

Since our goal is to train our minds to think positively and respond to situations in faith and love, we need to avoid any negative statements on our recordings. For example, instead of saying, "I will not smoke" it is more productive and effective to say, "I am smoke free." There are several reasons to strictly adhere to this rule. The first is that our brains do not process negative words as commands. Avoid words such as:

> Not
> won't
> will not
> do not
> don't
> can't
> can not

For reasons that are still in the stages of research, our brains simply skip over the negative words. So in the example, "I will not smoke," your brain actually only hears the words, "I" and "smoke," and then continues to create the desire in your body and your mind to smoke in order to carry out your command. Whereas, if you say, "I am smoke free" - your brain hears and processes the command to be free of smoke. I personally used this affirmation along with others to finally quit smoking. After 37 years as a pack a day smoker, I had tried to quit smoking so many times that I lost count. I had tried the patches, the gum, etc. Nothing worked for me until I put these affirmations on my recording and created a new stronger neural connection in my brain. This new connection or track in my brain gave me the ability to activate my faith and rely on God's power to keep me smoke free. This is how God designed our brains to work.

The second reason for avoiding negative statements is

that you have a choice to speak either fear or faith into and over your life. Remember that we learned earlier how thoughts are real things. In Chapter 2, we saw how thoughts carry electrical energy and have an effect on neural connections. The question is really a very simple one. Would you rather believe that life is meaningless and empty, or happy and fulfilling?

"Death and Life are in the power of the tongue"

Proverbs 18:21

Do you want to speak death (negative) or life (positive) into your brain? The choice is yours.

Spiritual Health

In any 12-step program, the second step discusses spirituality and the need to believe in something outside of ourselves. To begin the journey of spiritual growth, it is necessary to believe in a God that we can understand. For some of us that is a difficult process in the beginning. When I first began my journey in recovery, I did not want anything to do with religion of any kind. People calling themselves Christians had mentally and emotionally beaten me up with the Bible. There were deep scars on my mind and my heart with thick walls surrounding both. If I saw a Christian approaching me, especially one holding a Bible, I ran the other way – fast. To me, God was an angry old man, sitting up there somewhere in the invisible realm, with a book writing down everything I said and did. He was just waiting for the chance to lower the hammer and smash me to bits.

As I began working the steps with my sponsor, Yvonne, she told me I could borrow her God. I thought the roof was going to fall in when she said that, and I was just waiting for the lightening bolt to strike in the middle of her living room! I was shocked and had never heard of such a thing, but that is where I began.

She gently and slowly led me to a belief in a God that felt safe. Over time, that belief became a solid foundation on which I could build a life of spiritual growth. The longer I stayed sober and clean, the closer to God I became. Eventually, I was able to start reading the Bible again without feeling condemned. I began by only reading some of the Psalms and Proverbs, slowly over time reading more books of the Bible.

Yvonne helped me form an image of Jesus as a good-looking guy, riding up on a white Harley Davidson motorcycle to take me for a ride. I can hear some of you gasping – but it was not sacrilegious, it was the only thing I could comfortably relate to at that time in my life. It was the perfect starting point for me.

After a time, it was actually the Christian women in the meeting rooms of my recovery program that led me back to an intimate relationship with Jesus. They did not preach at me, beat me over the head with the Bible, or act self-righteous by looking down at me. They just loved me for who I was at that point in my life. Unconditionally, without expectations or demands.

Over the last 26 years, I have come a very long way and I can tell you for a fact that Jesus is my very best friend today and my constant companion. Today, in addition to my recovery program, I talk to the Lord every day – all day, read the Bible, and am a member of a local church and attend regularly.

The point is you need to begin wherever you are at now. If you struggle with the idea of God for whatever reason, then try saying this simple prayer every day for the next 90 days and keep your eyes open:

"God, please reveal yourself to me as you really are"

If you miss out on an intimate relationship with God as your loving Father, you are missing out on one of the best and most rewarding relationships that life has to offer. If you miss out on an intimate relationship with Jesus, you are missing out on the very best friend you could ever have. If you miss out on being filled with the Holy Spirit, you are missing out on the most intelligent and brilliant source of wisdom that ever existed.

In fact, there is actual science to prove that certain neurons in your brain fire when you meditate on God. In a book called, "How God Changes Your Brain" our brains are found to have a God Neuron. Dr. Newberg and Mr. Waldman (2009) explain this as:

We all begin with a simple neural circuit that captures our earliest impressions of God, and as we associate new meanings and qualities, these circuits interconnect, becoming larger and more complex over time (102).[3]

Have you ever noticed how good you feel when you listen to or sing along with a hymn or praise song to God? We feel good because we are doing what we are naturally designed to do, spending intimate and quality time with our Creator.

Mental and Emotional Health

For many of us that have suffered from trauma, addictions, and/or any type of mental illness the reality is that we do our thinking from our feelings most of the time. We are impulsive or compulsive or both. Our emotions control most of our decisions in every area of our lives. If it feels good, we do it repeatedly, without considering the risks or the consequences. Take for example someone who loves to play the slot machines. Most normal people may play a few dollars for fun and then walk away, but the person ruled by their emotions may sit there for hours, sinking money into the machine because they become drawn in by the excited feeling of winning. They cannot bear to tear themselves away from the machine because the next pull might be the one that triggers a win. Sadly, many such people burn through all the money in their bank accounts, seeking the next win and have nothing left to live on by the time they have to leave the machine.

The use of a personal recording can and does make a difference in affecting thought and behavior. It helps us to learn to stop and think things through BEFORE we make a decision or take any action.

Early on in my sobriety, my sponsor taught me a basic concept that bears repeating here.

In the words of Yvonne Porter, we need to:

I: Intellect

Put the I over the E   E: Emotions

We can include statements on our recording like, "I think before I act," and, "I consider all of the possible outcomes before making a decision." Does this mean we are going to act perfect from here on out for the rest of our lives? No, but if we are using our recording every day we are going to see a definite drastic improvement over time.

Name It and Claim It Doesn't Work

One of the concepts we need to discuss regard to a personal recording is, the idea of remaining realistic and staying within the bounds of the natural realm. An absurd example would be one in which God created me to be a fish, but I spent my whole life living in misery because I wanted to be a bear. I may as well accept the fact that it is physically impossible for me to go from being a fish to being a bear. It is outside of the natural laws of the universe. Now maybe in the very far distant future, when scientists learn to manipulate molecular biology with the application of Quantum Physics and new technology ... just kidding! Today, it is not possible, so I had better accept that life as a fish can be wonderful and the world of water I live in holds infinite possibilities for happiness.

"Name It and Claim It" is a term used to identify a certain theology taught by some televangelists and radical theologians. This view states that if I want any desire to come true, all I have to do is to is say it and believe its mine. VOILA!

There are several reasons that this philosophy does not work, and several ways in which this practice wanders from the practice of actual faith that the Bible teaches.

First, as in the example above, I am bound by natural laws that God put into place when He created the world. One natural law is that as a human being, I cannot fly without some type of equipment or mechanical assistance. I can shout the words "I CAN FLY – IN JESUS NAME I CAN FLY" from the rooftop of my house all day until I am blue in the face, but if I jump off my roof – the reality is that I will probably be killed or break both my legs. Now, IF God wanted to perform a miracle and give me the ability to fly, He could do that. He can do anything because he is God. However, the actual real probability of Him doing that is close to nil. It just will not happen. Why? Because it would not serve any good purpose. It would not glorify Him. It would only cause confusion and disorder.

God is all about order and creating harmony out of disharmony. That is one reason why He is so good at taking our chaotic messes and straightening them out and putting everything right again. If God has blessed me with a natural talent for creating beautiful artistic paintings, but I moan and complain because I cannot sing like Celine Dion – then not only am I wasting my life and my talent, I am insulting God and making myself needlessly miserable. What I would need to do, is to paint like there is no tomorrow because that is where my natural ability lies. That is where God can bless my life and guide me to find true happiness and fulfillment. That is where He can use me to bless others and bring joy into their lives.

Second, this type of philosophy does not put the main focus on God, but on self. Anything that tries to magnify the self is doomed to failure from the beginning. Anyone remember Satan? Why did he fall from grace and get his tail kicked out of heaven? Because he wanted to be equal with God. He was jealous of God and wanted the same power and glory. Bad Idea!

In the book used by Alcoholics Anonymous (2001) there is a section that talks about living to please oneself:

> The first requirement is that we be convinced that any life run on self-will can hardly be a success. On that basis, we are almost always in collision with something or somebody, even though our motives are good. Most people try to live by self-propulsion. Each person is like an actor who wants to run the whole show; is forever trying to arrange the lights, the ballet, the scenery and the rest of the players in his [or her] own way ... Selfishness – self-centeredness! That we think, is the root of our troubles. Driven by a hundred forms of fear, self-delusion, self-seeking, and self-pity ...(pg 61-62).[4]

When the main focus of our lives is living to please ourselves, glorify ourselves, or feed our ego – whether we know it or not we are headed for a fall. We live in this world with other people. By our very nature, we are born to be sociable creatures with an emotional need for love and companionship. This includes giving and receiving love. Think about it. When you look at a little baby and you make a funny face or a funny sound and as a result the baby is looks back at you with delight in their eyes and laughs or giggles. How does that make you feel? If you are like most people, you get a warm fuzzy feeling inside that goes all the way down to your toes! Why? Because you just shared your love with that beautiful and wonderful little person. Our very nature necessitates that we care for others, and be concerned about the welfare of those around us, such as family and friends. In order to truly care for and love those around us, it is necessary to deny selfish desires and ego feeding propositions. To do that without God is impossible. We must look to Him to help us deny self-centeredness and to love others.

Third, 'Name It and Claim It' puts the emphasis on the individual knowing what is good for his or her life. It creates a type of illusion that any one person can be all-knowing, all-wise, and have an ability to look into the future. Not only is this type of thinking extremely destructive and dangerous for the individual, it is a definite set-up for failure.

In the same way that we as parents would immediately take away a sharp knife from a little child, God our loving Father, often protects us from harm by removing situations or people from our lives that can be dangerous. I can't even count the number of times that I have prayed and begged God to bring something in my life, only to realize later that I am glad He didn't. Garth Brooks sings a song called "Thank God for Unanswered Prayers." I love that song because it reminds me that God is my loving Father. It reminds me that I can trust Him to always protect me.

"Sometimes Rejection - is God's Protection"

Joyce Meyer

We cannot see into the future. God can. Even if I had a crystal ball that would allow me to see what is going to happen tomorrow, I would immediately smash it with a sledgehammer until nothing was left but dust. Why? Because I trust God. Just as a child holds hands with their mother or father when crossing a busy street, trusting that their parent gets them safely across the street without harm, I trust that God guides me in the best possible way to handle whatever tomorrow brings.

Does that mean we cannot have goals, dreams, and aspirations and strive to achieve those? No. It simply means that we need to stay within the realm of reality and avoid fantasy. A good way to keep yourself grounded is to consult with your therapist, counselor, pastor, spiritual leader, or doctor when defining the things you would like to have in your future.

Personal Warning

I want to share with you a personal warning as to why the 'Name It and Claim It' philosophy should be avoided. As I stated above, we do not always know what is good for ourselves and what is not. God does. When we rely on His guidance and wisdom, we can avoid situations that are not beneficial for others or ourselves.

At one point in my past, there was a man that I started to notice. It all began very innocently. At first, he was just someone that made me smile. Someone that I admired for his achievements. I wrote him a poem that I hoped would be seen as an expression of my admiration. A simple non-romantic poem. Through the grapevine, I heard that he really liked it and appreciated the gesture. Then I wrote him another one, and another, and another. Each poem became a little more intimate and a little more romantic. He was delighted and seemed to enjoy the attention.

I really believed I had found my soulmate, and I used my recording to try to speak our future into existence. I told myself that I was operating out of faith and that this was God's will. I prayed that God would bring us together. On my recording, I put statements that: referred to us as a married couple, described how we interacted with each other, and described virtually every aspect of our lives together. The problem was that when I started recording these things, we had not even dated yet. My heart was sincere and I had the purest of motives. I really believed that I loved him deeply and that he loved me. He tried to reach out to me in his own way. He had some psychological problems and so did I in the areas of trust and relationships. Everything he did, did not work because it did not compute with my brain. Everything I did, did not work because it was not what he needed or wanted. The relationship or I should say the beginnings of a relationship, quickly became a circle of insanity for both of us. He was trying to get what he needed from me – mentally and emotionally. I was trying to get what I needed from him – mentally and emotionally. It turned out to be one huge disaster. There were emotional walls that neither of us could cross for many reasons. He and I both ended up experiencing a great deal of pain, rejection, and confusion. Not only that, but my faith took a heavy blow for quite awhile. In the beginning, I had begged God to open my eyes to really see him and let us be deeply in love. In the end, I begged God to help me forget I ever noticed him in the first place.

The reality here is that we cannot play God in our lives or someone else's life. When we try, we get hurt and cause others to get hurt. I caused a tremendous amount of emotional pain for this man and myself by using the power of this recording tool in the wrong way. Instead of asking God for His will, I was telling God what I thought His will ought to be and I paid a deeply painful price for it.

Please, do not make the same mistake! If you think you are in love with someone you have just recently met, take the time to set your mind on establishing a friendship first. If I had looked at this man in the beginning as just a friend instead of a soulmate or lifetime partner, I would have seen the areas of our lives where we were on different ground. The reality of the fact that we could be friends, but not partners would have been crystal clear to me and it would have saved us both a great deal of pain. So please consider this carefully, and **do not** put affirmations on your recording regarding a potential partner until you are sure that you are compatible with someone, that you have a solid foundation to build a relationship upon, and you have discussed a future together with the other person.

Using Emotions as you are Recording

One of the most powerful ways to tap into your mind's ability to change your thinking and behavior is to associate your affirmations with emotions. God created us to be emotional creatures. We love to get excited and yell and scream at football games, basketball games, or any type of sports. It feels good to let our emotions out and cheer on our favorite team or athlete. We are almost floating on air after we see a good comedy show, or watch a movie that made us laugh so hard it brought tears to our eyes. On the other end of the spectrum, most of us know how good we feel after we allow ourselves to have a good cry occasionally. We feel cleansed and lighter because we have emptied out all of that negative emotion.

Emotions are powerful. Medical studies have proven the link between negative emotions and disease. Many people are familiar with the old adage that if you do not stop worrying, you are going to give yourself an ulcer. In fact, many studies point to the reality that internalized anger, bitterness, and resentment over a number of years can result in or contribute to severe headaches, ulcers, cancer and a number of other debilitating illnesses.

Think about the effect that emotions have when you are trying to listen to others. Have you ever tried to listen to a lecture or speech given by someone who speaks in a monotone voice? There is no emotion, no variation in tone or pitch, just one level that sounds like a robotic voice. This type of speech is very difficult to listen to for any length of time. The mind's reaction is to wander; paying less attention to the speaker the longer, he or she talks. Alternatively, think about a time when you listened to someone who was full of energy and animated, maybe told a joke and had the entire audience laughing. When we hear a speaker with feelings and strong emotions, all of our senses become engaged in the moment and we hang on every word waiting to see what is next.

Your mind works the same way. We already learned that your brain has the ability to recognize its own voice and assign that a top priority. When we couple that with strong emotions, we are maximizing our impact of the messages we send to our mind. For example, the following affirmations would carry the most impact if you can say these with excitement and strong feeling:

"I am a strong, resilient, and confident woman (or man)"

"I love and accept myself exactly as I am"

I realize this is an extremely difficult thing to do for anyone suffering from depression, fatigue, or the doubt that this process may work for you. However, do the best you can to try to bring some emotion into your recording. If you ever wanted to be an actor or actress, you can pretend you are playing a role as you record your affirmations. Or you can trick your mind by pretending that you are speaking to a sad child that you are trying to cheer up when recording. If you still cannot seem to get any emotion going, just do the best you can. You can always do it better when you create an updated recording.

Updating Your Recording

In the same way that our lives change over time, we need to change and update our recordings periodically. One set of affirmations I had on my recording centered on school such as: turning in my assignments on time, reading and studying in advance vs. cramming everything in at the last minute, participating in class discussions, seeing myself with my diploma, etc.

Once I received my degree, it would be silly and impractical for me to continue to listen to that set of affirmations because it no longer applied to my life.

A good practice that I follow in the use of my recording is to re-record my affirmations every 6 months to a year, depending on what is going on in my life. I work from a written script, deleting what no longer applies to my life, and adding my current goals and/or dreams. There are always new affirmations and positive statements to add because life is always changing and so are we. As they say in meetings, "More will be revealed."

The workbook section includes a review of the highlights discussed here and suggestions for updating your recording.

Chapter 4 - References

1. Kaplan, J., Aziz-Zadeh, L., Uddin, L., & Iacoboni, M. (2008). The self across the senses: an fMRI study of self-face and self-voice recognition. Social Cognitive and Affective Neuroscience, 2008 3(3):218-223: doi:10.1093/scan/nsn014. The Author, Oxford University Press, Oxford Journals. http://iacoboni.bol.ucla.edu/pdfs/SCAN_Kaplan_v3p218.pdf

2. Meyer, Joyce. "Change Your Words, Change Your Life" (2012). New York: Faith Words, Hachette Book Group, Inc. pgs. 6-7. print.

3. Newberg, Andrew M.D. and Mark R. Waldman. "How God Changes Your Brain." (2009) Ballantine Books, Random House , Inc. pg. 102. print.

4. Alcoholics Anonymous (4th ed). (2001). New York: Alcoholics Anonymous World Services, Inc.. print.

Illustrations

1. Human Brain by Dream Designs / Free Digital Photos.net
http://www.freedigitalphotos.net/images/Human_body_g281-Human_Brain_p53797.html

A GOOD BRAIN WASHING

"Mountain Sunrise" by M-Pics / Free Digital Photos.net [1]

"Finally, brothers, whatever is true, whatever is noble, whatever is right, whatever is pure, whatever is lovely, whatever is admirable--if anything is excellent or praiseworthy-- think about such things."

Philippians 4:8 (NIV)

Chapter 5:
METHODS AND MUSIC IN A PERSONAL RECORDING

The method you use to record and the music you choose to play in the background have an impact on the success of your efforts. You need to choose a method that you are comfortable using. Likewise, you want to make sure that you choose music that is soothing to you.

Record in a Quiet Undisturbed Environment

An important point to remember is that when you are ready to record, find a quiet place to be alone. Preferably, a room where you can shut the door and not be disturbed. Where you will not run the risk of a partner, roommate, or children making fun of you and teasing you about what you are doing. We have already been through enough difficulties in our lives and faced many struggles, so let's make this process as easy as is humanly possible in order to insure our success.

If you live in a dormitory or find it difficult to get to a quiet place where you will not be disturbed, you can go to a public or college library. Most libraries have a small room that you can reserve for an hour or two. I have found these rooms to be very quiet and great for concentration. If all else fails, you can always take a laptop or cassette recorder, drive to a quiet park, and create your recording in your car.

Recording Methods

There are two ways to create your personalized recording. You can use your computer with recording software and a microphone, or you can use a cassette recorder. Make sure to choose the method that you are most comfortable with using so you can enjoy the process. The important thing to remember is to choose a method that allows you to listen to your recording at night and in the morning. So choose a method that is convenient and works for your lifestyle.

Computer Recording

If you are using a computer to create your recording make sure, you have a microphone plugged in to your hard drive, and that it is working properly. Next, make sure you have a voice recording software program. If you do not have one already, I recommend Audacity (see recommended websites in the back of the book). This program is available as a free download. The web site includes a help page, the ability to download a manual with step-by-step instructions, and a phone number if you need to contact the support staff. You can also enter your email address to be notified of program updates. This is the program I used to make my most recent personalized recording.

Make sure you have a blank recordable CD (CD-R) that you can place in your disk drive. Memorex produces good CD's that seem to last a long time and have high sound quality, but you can use any brand that you prefer.

Unless you are very tech savvy and know how to dub in background music (which I do not), you need to have another CD player near your desk or computer. This is for playing the background music while you are recording your affirmations. In order for the music to be picked up by your microphone, you have to do some experimenting and fine-tuning with adjusting the volume controls. Fortunately, this is very easy to do with the Audacity program. I suggest recording a few statements with your music playing in the background, and then playing back the recording to see how it sounds to you. This allows you to make adjustments before you get too far into your affirmations script.

Cassette Recording

As an alternative, if you feel more comfortable using a cassette recorder, do not worry if it seems old fashioned. A recording on cassette tape is still just as effective as a CD. In fact, until recently I had been using my cassette recorder for the past decade. I liked the idea of caring it with me on my morning walk, and then setting it on the nightstand by my bed.

When using a cassette recorder for your personalized recording, you want to purchase cassette tapes that are at least 60 to 90 minutes in recording time (30 to 45 minutes to each side). You have to record your affirmations on each side of the tape. This is more for convenience, because it allows you to simply flip the tape over for your daily listening instead of wasting time rewinding.

As with the computer recording, you need another music player beside you when you are recording your affirmations in order to play your background music. You also need to begin with a few affirmations, and then playback your recording to see where your volume controls need to be adjusted both on the recorder and the music player. You want the recording of both to be at a comfortable listening level.

Importance of Music in the Background of your recording

Music has played an important role in human history since the beginning of time. Ancient tribes played drums while warriors danced around fires to psych themselves up for the battle ahead. For centuries, mothers have sung their babies to sleep with soft melodies. Many of people around the world listen to a variety of soothing music to relax and get rid of stress. Classical music has been proven to increase the brain's ability to learn. In his book called "The Mozart Effect", Don Campbell provides readers with a condensed version of research from around the world. He points out that the beneficial effects of listening to certain types of music include improved efficiency of the brain, as well as a notable increase in creativity and clarity.[1]

Researchers have studied the effects of music on the brain for decades. In one recent study, the researchers were able to see visual proof of the brain's activity in response to music. They found that "rhythmic sound synchronizes brain waves." One of the researchers, psychologist Annett Schirmer stated, "within a few measures of music your brain waves start to get in synch with the rhythm."[2]

In order to make your personalized recording as effective as possible, you need to record music playing in the background as you are recording your affirmations. Due to the effects on the brain and the goal of creating stronger neural connections in the brain for success, you must limit your choice of music to an instrumental selection that is soothing, calming, and relaxing. Do not pick any music with words as that defeats the purpose. This is the reason why a radio station does not work. You do not want your brain to hear a DJ or anyone else on your recording. You want your brain to hear your words only.

One of my favorite selections for my recording is Native American flute music. For me, it not only relieves my stress by making me feel calm, it helps me create a visual image of God's beautiful creation as I listen, i.e. the mountains, the trees, eagles flying, soft clouds, etc. You need to choose music that works for you. Each one of us is different, so choose music that makes you feel peaceful and happy. If you are not sure what to choose, try listening to different types of music and see which ones fits your tastes. Some suggestions are classical, Native American flute music, sounds of nature, soft worship instrumentals, etc.

Visualization

As you are listening to your recording, picture your success. This practice reinforces the commands that you are giving your brain and activates your faith. Suppose one of your affirmations is to be healthy. Then as you hear your voice speaking that statement or set of statements, picture yourself actively taking part in a healthy activity. Maybe it is running, exercising, swimming, or yoga. See yourself happily engaging in that activity with as many details as you can. What are you wearing? What does the room look like? The more details you can add the better.

When I was in my last year of college, I was really struggling to keep going and not allow myself to quit. On my recording, I put affirmations surrounding my graduation. As I heard myself speaking those statements, I pictured myself in a cap and gown. I pictured the sky as blue with a few white puffy clouds. I pictured hearing my name and walking across the stage to get my diploma. I pictured holding my diploma in my hand. What this essentially did for me was to give me the ability to keep putting one foot in front of the other and to keep my eyes on the goal. Every time I the thought of giving up entered my mind, I immediately saw the picture in my mind of me as a graduate, because I had trained my mind to think that way. It works! I graduated and the sky was blue! ;)

Best Times to Listen

The best time to listen to your personalized recording is at night, just as you settle into bed and are ready to fall asleep. The two main reasons as to why this is the most effective time to listen are that music has been proven to help induce sleep and your brain is most open to your voice commands as you are drifting off to sleep.

There are numerous studies on the effects of music as an aid to inducing sleep. One study by de Niet et al. (2009) noted that "music-assisted relaxation can be used without intensive investment and training … [is] easily available and can be used by nurses to promote music-assisted relaxation to improve sleep quality." [3] Another more recent study proved the benefits of this practice to patients in intensive care units. Ryu, Park and Park (2012) found that "nurses working at [a] cardiac care unit can use music to improve sleeping in clients with percutaneous transluminal coronary angiography." [4] Since medical staff are using music to induce sleep in order to promote healing and health, we should be using this important method to promote health and healing every night as we prepare to go to sleep.

If you share a bed with another person then you want to make sure to use earphones. The reason listening as you are going to sleep is most effective, is because as you begin to relax into sleep, your mind is open and able to absorb your voice commands more than at any other time. Usually this is a time when there are no distractions or outside interferences competing for your attention. At first, this process may seem a little annoying or irritating for those of you who do not like listening to your own voice, but stick with it. Over time, this changes. Think of it as if your brain is a child that you need to train to stay in bed and go to sleep.

Another plus to making this a nightly habit is that after a short time your brain understands that this is a signal or cue to induce sleep without effort. This is especially helpful for people who have trouble falling asleep.

The next important time to listen to your recording is when you first wake up. You want to give your brain your commands and affirmations before the day's distractions have a chance to bombard your mind. This accomplishes several key factors. First, it activates your faith. Second, it sets the tone and mood for you to have a good day by instructing your mind to look at the glass of life as half full instead of half empty. Third, it reminds you to keep yourself open to new possibilities and opportunities that may cross your path during the day.

Conclusion

This is a process, a tool that works. It takes time. In today's world, we expect instant gratification. We have instant access to the internet. Instant access to each other with cell phones. We do not have the "instant" means to change brain and body structure in a healthy manner.

If you expect to instantly change your life overnight with this tool, you are setting yourself up for failure. It takes time to create stronger connections between neurons. It takes time to undo the damage that life events or your own destructive thinking has done to your brain. You must be persistent and patience while continuing to use this on a daily basis. Re-training your brain and changing established behavior patterns takes time and continued effort.

As I stated in the introduction, I was once helpless and hopeless. Even after several years in recovery, no matter what I tried, I continued to struggle in my life until I began using this recording on a daily basis. As a result of using this tool, my life and quality of recovery changed dramatically. Today, I am a completely different woman than I was ten years ago. I have seen this tool work successfully in my own life and I know it will work for you if you are willing to use it and be persistent and patient.

Chapter 5 - References

1. Campbell, Don. "The Mozart Effect" (2001). New York: Harper Collins Publishers, Inc.
http://www.mozarteffect.com/

2. Fields, R. Douglas (2012). The Power of Music: Mind Control by Rhythmic Sound. *Scientific American, Guest Blogs*, (2012/10/19).
http://blogs.scientificamerican.com/guest-blog/2012/10/19/th-power-of-music-mind-control-by-rhythmic-sound/

3. de Niet G., Tiemens B., Lendemeijer B., Hutschemaekers G. (2009). Music-assisted relaxation to improve sleep quality: meta-analysis.. Gelderse Roos Mental Health Care, Institute for Professionalization, Wolfheze, Netherlands. Journal of Advanced Nursing, 2009 Jul;65(7):1356-64. Epub 2009 Apr 28.
http://www.ncbi.nlm.nih.gov/pubmed/19456998

4. Ryu, MJ, Park JS, Park H (2012). Effect of sleep-inducing music on sleep in persons with percutaneous transluminal coronary angiography in the cardiac care unit. Keimyung University, DongSan Hospital, Daegu, South Korea. Blackwell Publishing Ltd. Journal of Clinical Nursing, 2012 Mar;21(5-6):728-35. Doi: 10.1111/j.1365-2702.2011.03876.x Epub 2011 Nov 15.
http://www.ncbi.nlm.nih.gov/pubmed?term=effect%20of%20sleep-inducing%20music%20on%20sleep%20in%20persons%20with%20percutaneous

Illustrations

1. *"Mountain Sunrise" by M-Pics / Free Digital Photos.net*
   http://www.freedigitalphotos.net/images/Sunset_And_Sunrise_g108-Mountain_Sunrise_p37009.html

Appendix A – Brain History Timeline

Milestones in Neuroscience Research
by Dr. Eric H. Chudler

Washington University, History of Neuroscience, Faculty pages.

http://faculty.washington.edu/chudler/hist.html

Used with permission.

Note: This is only a partial list taken from the above web site. For a full list see above web site.

4000 B.C.	Euphoriant effect of poppy plant reported in Sumerian records
1700 B.C.	Edwin Smith surgical papyrus written. First written record about the nervous system
460-379 B.C.	Hippocrates discusses epilepsy as a disturbance of the brain and states that the brain is involved with sensation and is the seat of intelligence
387 B.C.	Plato teaches at Athens. Believes brain is seat of mental process
335-280 B.C.	Herophilus (the "Father of Anatomy"); believes ventricles are seat of human intelligence
280 B.C.	Erasistratus of Chios notes divisions of the brain
177 B.C.	Galen lecture *On the Brain*

900	Rhazes describes seven cranial nerves and 31 spinal nerves in *Kitab al-Hawi Fi Al Tibb*
1000	Alhazen compares the eye to a camera-like device
1402	St. Mary of Bethlehem Hospital is used exclusively for the mentally ill
1410	Institution for the mentally ill established in Valencia, Spain
1504	Leonardo da Vinci produces wax cast of human ventricles
1543	Andreas Vesalius publishes *On the Workings of the Human Body*
1549	Jason Pratensis publishes *De Cerebri Morbis*, an early book devoted to neurological disease
1562	Bartolomeo Eustachio publishes *The Examination of the Organ of Hearing*
1564	Giulio Cesare Aranzi coins the term *hippocampus*
1573	Constanzo Varolio is first to cut brain starting at its base
1621	Robert Burton publishes *The Anatomy of Melancholy* about depression

1658   Johann Jakof Wepfer theorizes that a broken brain blood vessel may cause apoplexy (stroke)

1681   Thomas Willis coins the term *Neurology*

1695   Humphrey Ridley publishes *The Anatomy of the Brain*

1696   John Locke writes *Essay Concerning Human Understanding*

1721   The word "anesthesia" first appears in English (in *Dictionary Britannicum*)

1749   David Hartley publishes *Observations of Man*, the first English work using the word "psychology"

1752   The Society of Friends establishes a hospital-based environment for the mentally ill in Philadelphia

1755   J.B. Le Roy uses electroconvulsive therapy for mental illness

1760   Arne-Charles Lorry demonstrates that damage to the cerebellum affects motor coordination

1774   Franz Anton Mesmer introduces "animal magnetism" (later called hypnosis)

1784   Benjamin Rush writes that alcohol can be an addictive drug

1792   Giovanni Valentino Mattia Fabbroni suggests that nerve action involves both chemical and physical factors

1809   Johann Christian Reil uses alcohol to harden the brain

1812   Benjamin Rush publishes *Medical Inquiries and Observations upon the Diseases of the Mind*

1817   James Parkinson publishes *An Essay on the Shaking Palsy*

1818   Library of the Surgeon General's Office established (later to become the Army Medical Library and then the National Library of Medicine)

1826   Johannes Muller publishes theory of "specific nerve energies"

1827   E. Merck & Company market morphine

1832   Massachusetts establishes a "State Lunatic Hospital" for the mentally ill

1836   Gabriel Gustav Valentin identifies neuron nucleus and nucleolus

1837   The American Physiological Society is founded

1838   Robert Remak suggests that nerve fiber and nerve cell are joined

1838   Theordor Schwann describes the myelin-forming cell in the peripheral nervous system ("Schwann cell")

1838   Jean-Etienne-Dominique Esquirol publishes *Des Maladies Mentales*, possibly the first modern work about mental disorders

1838   Napoleonic Code leads to the requirement of facilities for the mentally ill

1843   James Braid coins the term "hypnosis"

1847   American Medical Association is founded

1847   The American Association for the Advancement of Science is founded

1848   Phineas Gage has his brain pierced by an iron rod [and survived]

1853   William Benjamin Carpenter proposes "sensory ganglion" (thalamus) as seat of consciousness

1865   Otto Friedrich Karl Deiters differentiates dendrites and axons

1870   Ernst von Bergmann writes first textbook on nervous system surgery

1871   Weir Mitchell provides detailed account of phantom limb syndrome

1875   Richard Caton is first to record electrical activity from the brain

1876   David Ferrier publishes *The Functions of the Brain*

1878   The first Ph.D. with "psychology" in its title is given to Granville Stanley Hall at Harvard University

1878   Paul Broca publishes work on the "great limbic lobe"

1879   Wilhelm Wundt sets up lab devoted to study human behavior

1885   Hermann Ebbinghaus publishes *On Memory*

1886   Joseph Jastrow earns the first Ph.D. from the first formal PhD program in psychology at Johns Hopkins University

1887   Sergei Korsakoff describes symptoms characteristic in alcoholics

1887   The National Institutes of Health established

1888   William Gill describes anorexia nervosa

1890   William James publishes *Principles of Psychology*

1891   Wilhelm von Waldeyer coins the term *neuron*

1892   American Psychological Association formed

1894   Margaret Floy Washburn is the first woman to receive a Ph.D. (Cornell University) in psychology

1896   Emil Kraeplein describes *dementia praecox* [manic depression]

1897   Charles Scott Sherrington coins the term *synapse*

1900   Sigmund Freud publishes *The Interpretation of Dreams*

1902   Physiologist Ida Hyde is the first woman elected to the American Physiological Society

1902   Oskar Vogt and Cecile Vogt coin the term "neurophysiology"

1903   Ivan Pavlov coins the term *conditioned reflex*

1906   Golgi and Cajal-Nobel Prize-Structure of the Nervous System

1906   Sir Charles Scott Sherrington publishes *The Integrative Action of the Nervous system* that describes the synapse and motor cortex

1909   Karl Jaspers publishes *General Mental Illness*

1910   Emil Kraepelin names *Alzheimer's disease*

1911   Eugen Bleuler coins the term *schizophrenia*

1911   George Barger and Henry Dale discover norepinephrine (noradrenaline)

1912   Original formula for the intelligence quotient (IQ) developed by William Stern

1920   Society of Neurological Surgeons is founded

1920   Henry Head publishes *Studies in Neurology*

1920   John B. Watson and Rosalie Rayner publish experiments about classical conditioning of fear (Little Albert experiments)

1921   Hermann Rorschach develops the *inkblot test*

1922   Army Medical Library established (was the Library of the Surgeon General's Office)

1932   Edgar Douglas Adrian and Charles S. Sherrington share Nobel Prize for work on the function of neurons

1935   Ward C. Halsted establishes the first clinical neuropsychological laboratory in the United States

1935   Frederic Bremer uses cerveau isole preparation to study sleep

1936   Henry Hallett Dale and Otto Loewi share Nobel Prize for work on the chemical transmission between nerves

1937	James W. Papez develops "visceral theory" of emotion
1938	B.F. Skinner publishes *The Behavior of Organisms* that describes operant conditioning
1938	Albert Hofmann synthesizes LSD
1939	Nathaniel Kleitman publishes *Sleep and Wakefulness*
1946	President Truman signs the National Mental Health Act
1947	The American EEG Society is founded
1948	The World Health Organization is founded
1949	Walter Rudolph Hess receives Nobel Prize for work on the "Interbrain"
1949	John Cade discovers that lithium is an effective treatment for bipolar depression
1949	National Institute of Mental Health was formally established
1950	The National Institute of Neurological Disorders and Stroke established (it has gone through several name changes)
1951	MAO-inhibitors introduced to treat psychotics

1952   The Diagnostic and Statistic Manual of Mental
       Disorders (DSM) was published by the
       American Psychiatric Association

1956   National Library of Medicine named (was the
       Army Medical Library)

1957   The American Medical Association recognizes
       alcoholism as a disease

1963   John Carew Eccles, Alan Lloyd Hodgkin and
       Andrew Fielding Huxley share Nobel Prize for
       work on the mechanisms of the neuron cell
       membrane

1969   The Society for Neuroscience is formed

1970   Julius Axelrod, Bernard Katz and Ulf Svante
       von Euler share Nobel Prize for work on
       neurotransmitters

1974   National Institute on Drug Abuse established

1990   U.S. President George Bush declares the decade
       starting in 1990 the"Decade of the Brain"

1992   National Institute on Drug Abuse becomes part
       of the National Institutes of Health

2000   Arvid Carlsson, Paul Greengard and Eric
       Kandel share the Nobel Prize for their
       discoveries concerning signal transduction in the
       nervous system

Appendix B

Misc. Brain Discoveries from various sources

Note:
This is just a miniscule sampling of the extensive research currently being conducted in the area of neuroscience. If your study is not included in this brief list, please do not take offense as it would be impossible to include all of the important studies here. This list is meant to inspire curiosity so that each reader will want to know more and conduct their own research and educational journey.

Howard Hughes Medical Institute   March 08, 2001
Gene-Trapping Method Powers Discovery of New Brain-Wiring Signals
http://www.hhmi.org/news/tessier4.html

> Researchers have developed a powerful screening method to identify genes that produce proteins that guide the wiring of the trillions of connections in the mammalian brain. The technique enables scientists to identify new genes and to determine which genes are responsible for defects in brain wiring that are observed during development. The scientists believe that this technique is likely to accelerate the discovery of new molecules involved in axon guidance.

New York University, Office of Public Affairs   Apr 16, 2007
New Institute Established to Study Brain's Emotional Functions
http://www.nyu.edu/public.affairs/releases/detail/1562

> New York University (NYU) and the Nathan S. Kline Institute for Psychiatric Research (NKI) today jointly announced the establishment of the Emotional Brain Institute (EBI), a new research endeavor aimed at understanding the neuroscience of emotions and their impact on behavior. A multi-disciplinary group of researchers will investigate origins of emotion from the level of behavior to neural systems, cell activity, molecules, and genes.

Tarleton State University, Media Relations Feb 17, 2009
Educators taught seven discoveries from brain research at ESP series
https://www.tarleton.edu/scripts/press/display.asp?id=2590

> Discoveries from brain research that could revolutionize education were the focus of the third workshop in the Jim Boyd Effective Schools Project (ESP) development series at Tarleton State University on Jan. 23. His presentation focused on seven discoveries from brain research—chronic stress has a debilitating affect on the human body; emotions influence our brains and bodies; environments affect brain

structure; memory can be improved through good teaching in a positive environment; the human brain can grow new brain cells; social conditions have an impact on brain functioning; and every age period presents opportunities for brain development and also for susceptibility.

Brain Research Institute, UCLA   2009
BRI In Action
http://www.bri.ucla.edu/bri_action/

One particularly successful project has been the Joint Seminars in Neuroscience series, which brings 30 leading neuroscientists to UCLA every year. More than 200 scientists from 20 disciplines gather weekly to hear these distinguished lecturers, and also join smaller groups of scientists for more focused discussions. Alliances often take shape at "journal club" and "affinity group" meetings of faculty, students and postdoctoral researchers. The BRI also provides core facilities of specialized equipment and resources that many research groups share. All our efforts are focused on attracting people and resources to collaborative multidisciplinary neuroscience.

University of Alabama at Birmingham, UAB Magazine
2009
The Plastic Brain: Part 2, UAB Neuroscientists Stretch
the Boundaries of the Mind by Bob Shepard
http://www.uab.edu/uabmagazine/2009/may/plasticbrai
n2

> The brain, as we saw in last week's story, is
> "plastic" in the sense that it can reshape itself after
> injury. But the power of plasticity doesn't stop
> there, says David Sweatt, Ph.D., chair of the UAB
> Department of Neurobiology, director of the
> Evelyn F. McKnight Brain Institute, and Evelyn
> F. McKnight Endowed Chair for Learning and
> Memory in Aging. According to Sweatt, the brain
> is also able to strengthen the connections between
> neurons—and even make new neurons.

National Institutes of Health
NIH for Neuroscience Research
The Human Connectome Project
http://www.neuroscienceblueprint.nih.gov/connectome/

> The NIH Human Connectome Project is an
> ambitious effort to map the neural pathways that
> underlie human brain function. The overarching
> purpose of the Project is to acquire and share data
> about the structural and functional connectivity of
> the human brain. It will greatly advance the
> capabilities for imaging and analyzing brain
> connections, resulting in improved sensitivity,
> resolution, and utility, thereby accelerating
> progress in the emerging field of human
> connectomics.

RECOMMENDED READING LIST

Affirmations / Meditations
Bible – Psalms, Proverbs, or any favorite scriptures
The Bible Promise Book by Barbour & Co.
Come Away My Beloved by Francis J. Roberts
God Calling by A.J. Russell
God's Promises for every day by W. Publishing Group
Hebrew Bible – Psalms, Proverbs, or any favorite scriptures
Love Out Loud Devotional by Joyce Meyer
As Bill Sees It: The A.A. Way of Life by AA World
    Services
Twenty-Four Hours A Day by Anonymous (Author)
Daily Reflections by AA World Services
Worthy of Love by Hazelden

Brain Health & Research
Brain Longevity
    by Dharma Singh Khalsa, M.D. with Cameron Stauth
The Brain That Changes Itself: Stories of Personal
Triumph from the Frontiers of Brain Science
    by Norman Doidge, M.D.
Change Your Brain, Change Your Life
    by Daniel G. Amen, M.D.
How God Changes your Brain
    by Andrew Newberg, M.D. and Mark Robert Waldman

Brainwashing
Brainwashing: The science of thought control by
    Kathleen Taylor
Battle for the Mind by William Sargant
The Manipulated Mind: Brainwashing, Conditioning, and
    Indoctrinationg by Denise Winn
The Mind Field by Robert Ornstein, Ph.D.

Spiritual Growth

Approval Addiction by Joyce Meyer

Battlefield of the Mind book and Study Guide
  by Joyce Meyer

Came to Believe by AA World Services

Change Your Words, Change Your Life by Joyce Meyer

Divine Romance by Gene Edwards

Effective Prayer Life by Chuck Smith

Enjoying Where You Are on the Way to Where You are
  Going by Joyce Meyer

Evidence that Demands a Verdict by Josh McDowell

Experiencing God's Presence by Warren and Ruth Myers

Hinds Feet in High Places by Hannah Hurnard

Mountain of Spices by Hannah Hurnard

Root of Rejection by Joyce Meyer

Search for Serenity by Lewis F. Presnall

Search for Significance by Robert S. McGee

The Story of Job by Jessie Penn-Lewis

Straight Talk by Joyce Meyer

Miscellaneous

The Cinderella Complex by Colette Downing

The Greatest Saleman in the World by Og Mandino

The Power of Postive Thinking by Norman Vincent
  Peale

The Power of Your Subconcious Mind by Dr. Joseph
  Murphy

Self-Defeating Behaviors by Milton R. Cudney, Ph.D. and
  Robert E. Hardy, Ed.D.

Think and Grow Rich by Napolean Hilln

Why Do I Think I am Nothing Without A Man? by
  Penelope Russianoff, Ph.D.

RECOMMENDED WEB SITES

Amen Clinics
http://www.amenclinics.com/

Audacity
http://audacity.sourceforge.net/

CBN (Christian Broadcasting Network)
http://www.cbn.com/

Joyce Meyer Ministries
http://www.joycemeyer.org/

Dr. Oz
http://www.doctoroz.com/

Dr. Phil
http://www.drphil.com/

The Mozart Effect Resource Center
http://www.mozarteffect.com/

Regent University
http://www.regent.edu

INDEX

A GOOD BRAIN WASHING

*Take Control of Your Mind with a
Personalized Recording*

WORKBOOK SECTION

"Business Lady Writing On Notebook" by adamr /
Free Digital Photos.net [1]

"Study to shew thyself approved unto God, a workman that needeth not to be ashamed"
2 Tim 2:15 (KJV)

TABLE OF CONTENTS

Section 1:
REVIEW AND SUMMARY

The purpose of this workbook section is to prepare your list of affirmations for your personal recording. There are guidelines to follow in this process that are in line with the way God designed our brains to work.

First, we will review important points to remember and conclude with a summary as you prepare your affirmations for recording.

Review

In Chapter 1, we learned that there are many reasons behind the need to wash out our brains or renew our minds on a daily basis. The negative messages we have received from the time in the womb to adulthood will continue to haunt our conscious and unconscious minds until they are replaced or changed.

1. Negative thoughts have a powerful impact on ourselves, our relationships and every area of our lives. ˙

2. Negative thoughts rise to the surface and are expressed in the forms of mental illness, addictions, and/or health problems and diseases.

In Chapter 2, we learned the basic structure of the brain and how thoughts affect the brain.

1. Thoughts and feelings stimulate or repress certain neurotransmitters that have an effect on our actions and/or reactions.

2. Continual and repetitive listening and speaking positive statements strengthen neural connections resulting in mental and emotional health.

3. Mental and emotional health results in long-term physical health.

In Chapter 3, we learned the warning signs of mind control by others.

1. We saw how allowing ourselves to be easily influenced by others could result in harm to ourselves and affect all of those we love.

2. We saw that if any individual, group, or organization attempts to separate us from our family and friends – we need to get as far away

from them as quickly as possible.

In Chapter 4, we learned important information about this recording tool and guidelines to follow in preparation for recording.

1. The importance of listening to our own voice vs. someone's voice on a recording. We learned that the right side of the brain becomes highly active when hearing our own voice on a recording, making it a priority to our unconscious mind.

2. The necessity of avoiding negative statements in a recording.

3. The need to keep our statements within the bounds of reality.

4. We saw how this powerful tool, if misused could bring destruction and damage into our own life and hurt those around us.

5. That we need to use emotions in our voice when we record.

6. The need to periodically update and change your recording as your life changes.

In Chapter 5, we reviewed the mechanics of creating a recording.

1. The methods available for creating a recording,

computer microphone or cassette recorder.

2. The importance of choosing a recording method that fits your lifestyle.

3. The importance of playing instrumental music only in the background, while you are recording your affirmations.

4. The best times to listen to your recording.

Summary

This is an important life-changing tool that if used in the proper way, produces dramatic results. Each one of us is different. Where one person may begin to see and feel the results of using this recording in a few weeks, for another person it may take several months or longer.

BE PERSISTENT AND PATIENT

You will only receive the benefit equal to the amount of effort you are putting into using this recording on a daily basis. The choice is up to you. Either you want to get better and feel better or you do not. If you want to get better, have a higher quality of mental and emotional health, then put the effort into creating a good recording and use it every morning and night.

If you are not sure what statements to put on your recording, sit down with a pastor, counselor, physician, etc. and go over the examples in the following sections.

Circle or highlight the ones that apply to you, your life, and your goals.

This works. It has worked in my life to produce incredible results. I sincerely believe it will work for you if you use it.

Guidelines to Follow

1. Write or type your list of affirmations and statements on blank paper or a word document so you can read continuously once you begin recording.

2. Avoid negative words or statements such as "I won't (or will not)", "I don't (do not)", etc.

3. Be sure to address every area of your life: i.e. spirituality, identity, mental and emotional health, physical health, school/education, job/career, spouse, family, children, finances, hobbies, recreation, pets, future goals, etc.

4. Be realistic and stay within the bounds of your talents and skills or those you have a natural ability in which to excel.

5. Pick instrumental music that soothes you and is something you enjoy. Play it softly in the background as you record.

6. Record at a time and in a private place where you

will not be ridiculed, teased, or interrupted by someone else.

7. Protect your recording from others. If you share a room or house with others, put your recording in a safe place when you are not home, i.e. under lock and key. You do not want to leave yourself open to ridicule or teasing by another person. Even if it is meant in fun, it can still be hurtful.

8. If you share a bed, use headphones.

9. Use positive emotion in your voice as you are saying your statements.

10. Update your recording on a regular basis as your life changes or goals are met.

11. Record enough affirmations or statements to create a 30 to 45 minute recording. If you get to the end of your script, start from beginning and repeat your affirmations/statements again.

12. Continue to use your current support system, i.e. counseling, groups, meetings, etc.

Remember the examples on the following pages are suggestions, many of which came from my personalized recording. Use these as a guideline to create your own statements that apply specifically to your needs, goals, and life.

Section 2:
WORD LIST

The purpose of this section is to spark your imagination and get those creative pathways flowing in your brain. Use the word list to create positive statements for your recording. You can use these words for statements about yourself and for statements about others in your life, for example your children.

Some of you may feel uncomfortable using a statement such as "I am a wonderful person." When we feel bad about ourselves or are insecure for a long period of time, it does feel weird and strange to suddenly be saying something positive aloud. However, I strongly encourage you to push forward and say these statements anyway. Say them with as much conviction as you can and know that over time you will feel better and enjoy more peace inside.

In this section, your statements are confirming who you are, not as you may be now, but how you would like to see yourself, feel about yourself, or how you want to react to situations. You must make these statements as if these statements are already true. Pick as many items from the list below as you would like to have become a part of your identity.

You can also use these words to describe people you love for the family section. For example, "My spouse is thoughtful and considerate."

Descriptive words

Able	Assertive
Accepting	Attentive
Accountable	Attractive
Adaptable	Authentic
Adept	Balanced
Admirable	Beautiful
Adventurous	Believable
Alert	Benevolent
Ambitious	Bodacious
Amusing	Brave
Animated	Brilliant
Articulate	Calm
Artistic	Capable

Captivating	Dedicated
Careful	Dependable
Caring	Devoted
Cautious	Diplomatic
Charismatic	Disciplined
Charming	Dynamic
Cheerful	Eager
Clean	Easy-going
Clever	Educated
Communicative	Effective
Compassionate	Empathetic
Compatible	Encouraging
Competent	Engaging
Confident	Enjoyable
Considerate	Enterprising
Consistent	Entertaining
Convincing	Enthusiastic
Cooperative	Expressive
Courageous	Faithful
Courteous	Fascinating
Creative	Flexible
Credible	Forgiving
Dazzling	Forthright
Decisive	Friendly

Fruitful	Ingenious
Fun	Inspiring
Funny	Insightful
Generous	Integrity
Gentle	Intelligent
Genuine	Interesting
Good-Listener	Intuitive
Graceful	Inventive
Happy	Jovial
Hard-Working	Joyful
Harmonious	Just
Healthy	Kind
Helpful	Knowledgeable
Honest	Light-hearted
Honorable	Lively
Hospitable	Logical
Humble	Longsuffering
Humorous	Loving
Idealistic	Loyal
Imaginative	Magnanimous
Impressive	Marvelous
Independent	Masterful
Industrious	Mature
Influential	Merciful

WORD LIST

Methodical	Popular
Mindful	Positive
Modest	Powerful
Moral	Practical
Motivated	Precise
Natural	Prepared
Neat	Problem-Solver
Noticeable	Professional
Obedient	Prompt
Open-Minded	Proper
Optimistic	Punctual
Orderly	Rational
Organized	Realistic
Outgoing	Reasonable
Passionate	Receptive
Patient	Reflective
Peaceful	Relaxed
Perceptive	Reliable
Persevering	Resilient
Personable	Resourceful
Persuasive	Respectful
Playful	Responsible
Pleasant	Responsive
Polished	Righteous

Secure	Talented
Self-Confident	Tender
Self-Controlled	Tenderhearted
Self-Disciplined	Thorough
Self-Reliant	Thoughtful
Self-Restrained	Thrifty
Sensible	Tidy
Sensitive	Tolerant
Serene	Truthful
Sincere	Upbeat
Skilled	Understanding
Sociable	Uplifting
Soft Spoken	Useful
Spiritual	Valuable
Spontaneous	Versatile
Stable	Vibrant
Stimulating	Visionary
Strong	Vivacious
Stunning	Warm
Successful	Winner
Supportive	Wise
Surprising	Witty
Sympathetic	Wonderful
Tactful	Worthy

Section 3:
GENERAL AFFIRMATION EXAMPLES

It is important to address every area of your life when you are writing out your affirmations and positive statements. In order to grow mentally and emotionally and become as healthy as possible, we need to command our brains to function in healthy ways in every aspect of our lives.

There would be no sense in developing a positive identity, while holding on or continuing to live out destructive habits in other areas. It would be a waste of time.

For example, if you spent a great amount of effort in developing a healthy self-image, but continued to be a doormat to certain people such as a spouse or adult child in your life, you would end up under mining your efforts and wasting your time.

In order to make a complete and thorough personalized recording, affirmations and positive statements should be made about each of the following areas in this order:

1. Spirituality

2. Personal Identity

3. Personal Care

4. Health – Mental, Emotional, and Physical

5. Relationship with Spouse / Partner

6. Relationships with Family members

7. Finances

8. Education

9. Job / Career

10. Hobbies / Interests

11. Home Environment

12. Future Goals and Plans

Spirituality

If you struggle with the idea of God, know that it is okay to begin wherever you are at now. The important point is to begin to reach out. As was suggested earlier, you can start by saying this simple prayer for 90 days and keep your eyes open, "God please reveal yourself to me as you really are." Look over the example statements in this section and use the ones that you can accept now. You can always add to or change these later when you create a periodic update to your recording.

For those of you who are comfortable with a general concept of God, know that the point of this section is to deepen your relationship with God. The goal is to form a loving and intimate relationship with God, so intimate that:

1. you feel God's presence with you throughout your day.

2. you come to know God as your very best friend who will never leave your side.

3. you will know in this relationship that your God is your constant source of strength, comfort, peace, reassurance, security, and wisdom.

If you are Christian, go to Section 4 and use that section to increase your faith and intimacy with God.

If you are Jewish, use the Hebrew Bible to record your favorite passages and scriptures. You can also take the principles taught by Rabbi's to create personal statements that increase or deepen your faith.

If you are a member of a support group or a 12-step program, you can use daily readings or prayers found within their literature.

Do not ignore or skip over this area. We are human beings with 4 parts to your natural self: Spiritual, Mental, Emotional, and Physical. If you leave this area out of your recording, your unconscious mind realizes something is missing and you cheat yourself from realizing your maximum results.

~~~~~~~~~~~~~~~~~~~~~~~~~~~~~~~~~~

I spend quality time in meditation and prayer every day

I listen for and recognize the voice of my God

I obey my God's voice

I have an intimate relationship with my God

I trust my God completely

I realize my God is my best friend and constant companion

I find comfort, peace, reassurance, safety, and calmness in my God's presence

I grow closer to my God everyday

My God is loving, kind, patient, tolerant, gentle, strong, considerate, merciful, all wise, all knowing, all powerful, protective of me, rescues me, counsels me, guides me, accepts me and loves me completely exactly as I am today in this moment.

My God is always right beside me wherever I go and whatever I do.

My God has a wonderful sense of humor

My God fills me and my life with Joy and Laughter

My God feels everything I feel

My God wants me to be happy and whole

My God wants the best for me

My God believes in me

My God wants me to live a long healthy and happy life

My God has a good reason for everything that has happened or will happen in my life

My God has forgiven me for my past and future mistakes

My God has set me free

My God always has my best interests at heart

My God has a wonderful plan for my life

Personal Identity

I am a strong, resilient, and confident (man or woman)

I am a calm, thoughtful, and respectful (man or woman)

I am self-controlled and self-disciplined in all situations

I am a positive person

I am free from my past

I am peaceful inside and out

I am free from my past and responsive to my present

I am serene in the midst of trouble

I make wise decisions in every area of my life

I am intuitive and highly intelligent

I am insightful and knowledgeable

I am considerate and thoughtful to all those around me

I am patient in all situations

I am sympathetic to those in pain or in need

I dependable and responsible

I persevere in the face of adversity

I face fear and overcome it with courage

GENERAL AFFIRMATION EXAMPLES

I am a person of integrity

I am honorable

I am truthful and honest

I adapt to new situations quickly and comfortably

I am funny and have a great sense of humor

I am loving and kind to myself and others

I am loving and kind to all of God's creatures

I am stable and focused in all areas of my life

I am punctual and arrive at all my appointments on time

I am a winner

I am a worthwhile person

I am valuable and have much to contribute to others

I am worthy of giving and receiving love

I am relaxed and free of stress

I am free from fear and worry

I am a fascinating and interesting person

I am successful and creative

I am intelligent and a problem-solver

I see the good in everyone and in every situation

I am beautiful inside and out

I enjoy every moment of everyday

I uplift and encourage all those who cross my path everyday

I love and accept myself exactly as I am

I have a wonderful and divine sense of humor

I make others laugh at appropriate times

I am witty, intelligent, and wise

I am loyal, honest, and forthright

I am spontaneous

I am intuitive, insightful, and discerning

When I make a mistake, I immediately forgive myself and learn from the experience

I am talented and creative

I am filled with joy and a zest for life

I am well dressed and always look attractive

I am honest in all of my actions and words

When faced with a problem or crisis, I respond with

calmness and wisdom

When faced with a problem or challenge, my mind immediately focuses on solutions

My speech is clear and precise

I am witty

I am fun to be with - people around me enjoy my company

I fill my life with laughter and joy

Personal Care

Note

Some of these statements may seem ridiculous, however they should be included in your recording because they speak to the internal need of seeing ourselves as valuable and worthy of the best self-care possible.

~~~~~~~~~~~~~~~~~~~~~~~~~~~~~~~~

I shower or bathe at least once a day

I brush my teeth at lease twice a day

I wash my hair at least 3 times a week

I use deodorant and lotion to take care of my body everyday

I read something positive and encouraging everyday

I take the time to relax and enjoy my life

I always choose to wear comfortable clothing that enhances my appearance

I always choose to wear shoes that are comfortable and enhance my appearance

I am patience, kind, and considerate of my body and mind

I take the time to treat my body to a relaxing hot bath

with candlelight and soft music

I take the time to care for my hair, nails, and skin to maintain them in the best possible condition

I take the time to enjoy my favorite activities

I remind myself that I am valuable and worthy of taking good care of myself

Health – Mental, Emotional, and Physical

I am mentally, emotionally, physically, and spiritually healthy

I am mentally clear, balanced, focused, and stable

I am emotionally stable

I dwell on only positive thoughts and solutions to problems throughout the day

I eat healthy foods and find healthy foods delicious and satisfying

I eat plenty of fruits, vegetables, whole grains, dairy products, and meat every day

I eat a balanced diet every day

I drink 8 glasses of water or the equivalent in ounces of half my weight of water everyday

I exercise for 30 minutes everyday

I visit the doctor and dentist regularly to maintain a plan of maximum health

I know the limitations of my body and mind and stay within those limitations

I am free from disease or distress of any kind

I sleep a deep, peaceful, and restful sleep for at least 8

hours every night

I am free from all addictions

I am smoke free

My lungs are clear and strong

When a smoker lights a cigarette in front of me, I politely excuse myself and walk away

When tempted to smoke, I take slow deep breaths and chew a piece of gum or suck on a piece of sugar-free candy

I enjoy being smoke free reminding myself that I am practicing healthy living

All of my organs are strong and healthy

All of my muscles are toned, strong, and in perfect condition

My brain is healthy and functions perfectly

My weight remains between 130 to 135 pounds

My eyesight is perfect, clear, and sharp

My hearing is perfect

All of my senses are fully functioning at their highest capacity

I know the limits of my body and mind and I stay within

those limits

I choose only those behaviors and practices that are supportive of maintaining my body and mind in the healthiest way possible

I see myself as healthy and whole

I see myself living a long and purposeful healthy life

Relationship with Spouse / Partner

Note: You can use either "we" or "I" whichever you are most comfortable with for example if you choose to use "I", you would say "I love my (husband, wife, or partner) to the fullest possible extent, "I encourage my (husband, wife, or partner) to grow spiritually and spend time alone with God", "I have an emotionally healthy relationship with my (husband, wife, or partner)", "I am honest with my (husband, wife, or partner) and (he or she) is honest with me", etc.

~~~~~~~~~~~~~~~~~~~~~~~~~~~~~~~~

We love each other to the fullest possible extent

We encourage each other to grow spiritually and spend time alone and together with God

We continue to grow closer in friendship and intimacy every day

We have an emotionally healthy relationship

We have healthy boundaries in our relationship and we respect each other's boundaries

We allow each other the freedom to be independent of each other

We happily allow each other to spend time apart with each partner's own friends

We trust each other completely

We are honest with each other

We hold each other's secrets in the highest confidence

We share our most intimate thoughts and desires

We respect and honor each other at all times

We find comfort and security in each other's presence whether in silence or in communication

We allow each other to enjoy each partner's own activities and hobbies

We share our laughter, joy, tears, and pain

We comfort each other through difficult times

We actively and passionately pursue healthy lifestyles

We are patient and tolerant with each other

We focus on each other's positive qualities and choose to overlook each other's shortcomings

In the presence of others, we purposely treat each other with respect and honor, making only positive statements about each other

We treat each other with good manners at all times, always using "please" and "thank you" when appropriate

We believe in and support each other's goals, dreams, and

heart's desires

We encourage each other to excel in areas of personal interest

We are concerned for each other's welfare in all things

We find common ground and solutions to financial problems or challenges

We encourage each other to save money and spend money wisely

We are considerate, kind, tolerant, patient, and supportive of each others relatives

We maintain a unified position when it comes to interference in our relationship by others

We protect and defend each other in response to all outside influences and challenges

We respect each other's personal property

We respect each other's privacy

We always believe the best about each other

We encourage each other to read something positive and uplifting every day

We honor and support each other's likes and dislikes

Relationships with Family and Children

Note: you can name each child or family member individually or you can use a general term such as "my child", my children" or "my family"

You may wonder why you should include this section in your personalized recording. The reason is that you are activating your faith in believing for the best for the people you love. As we learned in Chapter 2, thoughts are real things which create energy in ourselves, in those around us, and in the world around us.

~~~~~~~~~~~~~~~~~~~~~~~~~~~~~~~~

My child has strong faith in and an intimate relationship with God

My (son, daughter, other relative) (name) is emotionally stable and mentally clear

My (son, daughter, other relative) (name) is strong and physically healthy

My child is highly intelligent

My children are well behaved and obedient

My child is well mannered

My child is creative and talented

My (son or daughter) studies diligently, completes all homework assignments on time, and is successful in school or college

My (son or daughter) is on the Honor Roll at school

My (son or daughter) has a wonderful personality

My (son or daughter) uses common sense and makes the right choices for life

My (son or daughter) is surrounded by good friends who make right choices

My (son or daughter) is an excellent (student, athlete, musician, etc.)

My (son, daughter) loves and enjoys (his or her) life

My (son, daughter) is considerate, kind, and compassionate

My (son, daughter) is an excellent (nurse, teacher, electrician, etc.)

My (son, daughter) has an excellent work ethic

My (mother, father, in-law) is emotionally stable and mentally clear

My (mother, father, in-law) is strong and physically healthy

My (mother, father, in-law) respects and honors my boundaries and my choices

My (mother, father, in-law) loves me and encourages me to do my best in life

My (mother, father, in-law) respects my wishes and guidelines with my children

My (mother, father, in-law) is prosperous and successful

My (mother, father, in-law) is surrounded by loving and supportive friends

My (mother, father, in-law) has an active social life

My (mother, father, in-law) takes part in and enjoys (hobbies and interests)

All members of my family and I are blessed in all our comings and goings

All members of my family and I are safe and protected by God's Angels at all times

All members of my family are healthy and full of energy

All members of my family think before taking any action and make right choices

All members of my family are open and honest with each other

All members of my family are nurturing and supportive of each other

All members of my family have healthy boundaries and

respect each other's boundaries

All members of my family make quality time to spend with each other

All members of my family are considerate and kind to each other

All members of my family practice good morals and values

At family gatherings, all members of my family are joyous and happy and thoroughly enjoy and value each other's company

Finances

I am a good steward

I tithe faithfully every time I receive money

I think carefully before I spend money making sure that I am spending wisely

I make a deposit in my savings account every time I get paid

I am thrifty with money in every area of my life

I pay all of my bills on time

I consider each purchase carefully and only spend money on things that are necessary

I have a healthy savings account

I am financially prepared for unseen circumstances

I am blessed and prosperous in all that I do

I follow a budget

I plan for and have money set aside for special events and vacations

I have money set aside for emergencies

I have money set aside for retirement

My home and vehicles are paid in full

My home and vehicles are in good repair and free of mechanical problems

I have life insurance policies in place on my self and every member of my family

I am generous and realize that as I bless others, I will be blessed

I donate to charities that I have researched and found to be valid

I am a wise shopper and find excellent bargains on all that I purchase

GENERAL AFFIRMATION EXAMPLES

Educational Goals

I am a successful student

I enjoy being in school and performing well

I arrive at my classes on time and well prepared for the day

I plan and organize my time effectively to allow maximum study time for all my classes

I complete my homework assignments before getting involved with other things

I enjoy studying and I comprehend what I study

I have the courage to ask questions of my teachers to gain a deeper understanding of the material in my classes

I have the courage and confidence to ask for help when I need it

I am well liked in school

I enjoy helping others with their homework

I am considerate and supportive of my classmates

I encourage my fellow students to do their very best

I actively participate in study groups or organize and begin a study group when needed

I maintain a good and positive working relationship with

my teachers or professors

I practice my (music, art, or sports activity) on a daily basis for at least one hour

I am a member of (school club, social organization, etc) and enjoy working with others

I focus only on making positive statements about my friends and fellow students

I am highly motivated to succeed and continue working hard to attain my (degree).

Job / Career Goals

I am a hard worker

I enjoy my work

I enjoy the people I work with and choose to focus on their positive qualities

I take pride in a job well done

I am a team player and encourage other members of my team

I respect and honor my supervisors and those in authority over me

I maintain a positive and helpful attitude at work

I arrive 15 minutes before my scheduled time and remain at work until 5 minutes after my scheduled time to leave

I take my breaks and lunch on time and return from my breaks and lunch on time

I show up at work everyday I am scheduled to be there without fail

I focus on solutions to problems and challenges in my work

I am creative and talented in my work

I am a natural born leader

I am organized and efficient

I plan ahead and complete all of my tasks on time

I am blessed and prosperous in my work

I take all necessary steps to advance in my chosen career

I maintain a professional attitude and dress in a professional manner at work

I keep my personal life separate from my work life

Hobbies and Interests

I make time to pursue my favorite hobbies

I enjoy (hobby or interest) and find it fulfilling

I enjoy (2nd hobby or interest) and find it fulfilling

I am creative and talented at (hobby or interest)

I am creative and talented at (2nd hobby or interest)

I enjoy networking with others that take part in (hobby or interest)

I am open to learning to new skills in (hobby or interest)

My (hobby or interest) is important to my fulfillment as a healthy individual

I enjoy sharing my (hobby or interest) with others

I find satisfaction and joy in my creativity

I am always thinking of new ideas and ways to improve my (hobby or interest)

I use my (hobby or interest) to help raise money for charitable organizations

I am a member of (organization of hobby or interest)

I attend meetings of fellow (hobby or interest)

I enjoy meeting new people associated with (hobby or

interest)

I enjoy teaching (hobby or interest) to others

I read books and watch programs about (hobby or
interest)

I stay within my financial budget when it comes to
spending money on my (hobby or interest)

Home Environment

My home is beautiful and safe

My home is peaceful, tranquil, and calm

My home is fully paid for and in good repair

My home is like a safe protected harbor in a stormy sea

My home is filled with precious treasures and memorabilia

My home is beautifully decorated and filled with new furniture

Each room in my home has its own personality and flavor

All of the appliances in my home are in good working condition and free of problems

My home has large picture windows with beautiful views

My home is clean and free of clutter

My home is well organized and well maintained

My home smells fresh and clean

Our backyard is filled with thick green grass, vibrant plants, and large shade trees

Our pool is surrounded by a safety fence

Our pool is filled with clean crystal blue water

Our pool is well maintained and in good repair

We have an ongoing good relationship with all of our neighbors

Our neighborhood is safe and well protected

When people enter our home they immediately have a sense of warmth and relaxation

Future Goals and Plans

I receive awards and scholarships to pay for my education

I have my (High School diploma, Associate's degree, Bachelor's degree, Master's degree, or Ph.D.)

I am graduating from (school) at the top of my class

My GPA is a 3.90

I am an Honor Roll Student

I receive a promotion and bonus as an (line of work or career)

My book is listed on the New York Times best selling list in the top ten books

My new CD or album just went Platinum

I am receiving the (the award for your career or interest)

I am skilled at (sport, personal interest, career, etc)

I am taking a trip to Hawaii in the summer of 2013

I am retiring from (career) at age (?)

I enjoy traveling and have the opportunity to travel in the U.S. and abroad

I am debt free

I have a savings account with $50,000.

I have a minimum balance of $5,000 in my checking account at all times

I have achieved success as a (dream or heart's desire)

I have built a successful ministry for (dream or heart's desire)

Section 4:
CHRISTIAN RELATIONSHIP WITH GOD AND IDENTITY IN CHRIST

My personal belief is that Jesus Christ is my Savior, Best Friend, Counselor, Rescuer, Protector, and the Center of my life. Therefore, the following meditations and affirmations are from my personal recording and have been gathered from various sources.

If you would like to have a relationship with Jesus Christ say this prayer aloud right now:

Dear God, I am sorry for my sins and ask you to forgive me and wash me clean. I need you in my life. I believe that your son Jesus Christ, shed His blood and died for me on the cross. I believe that you raised Him from the dead. I now believe that He is my Lord and my Savior and I ask you to fill me with the Holy Spirit. Thank you for giving me the gift of Eternal Life. Help me and guide me in Your Will. Amen.

An important part of your growth and maturity as a Christian is to read the Bible, God's Holy Word. Just as we have to eat food to sustain our bodies, we must read and absorb the Word of God to feed our spirit. Fellowship with other Christians is another important area in developing your relationship with Jesus. Ask the Lord to guide to the church where He would have you attend.

The following affirmations and positive statements have helped me to form a solid foundation for my faith. By putting these statements on my recording and listening to them everyday, they have helped me to grow and mature in Christ.

Relationship with The Lord Jesus Christ

I love the Lord my God with all of my Heart, all of my Soul, all of my Mind, and all of my Strength (Mark 12:30)

I love my neighbors (all people) as I love myself (Mark 12:31)

~~~~~~~~~~~~~~~~~~~~~~~~~~~~~~

Note:

The scriptures for **Identity in Christ** are used with permission and taken from the **Joyce Meyer Ministries Website.**
http://www.joycemeyer.org/articles/eaarchive.aspx ?tag=Christian_Living

IDENTITY IN CHRIST

I am complete in Him who is the Head of all principality and power (Colossians 2:10)

I am alive with Christ (Ephesians 2:5)

I am free from the law of sin and death (Romans 8:2)

I am far from oppression and fear does not come near me (Isaiah 54:14)

I am born of God and the evil one does not touch me (1 John 5:18)

I am holy and without blame before Him in love (1 Peter 1:16; Ephesians 1:4)

I have the mind of Christ (Philippians 2:5; I Corinthians 2:16)

I have the peace of God that passes all understanding (Philippians 4:7)

I have the Greater One living in me; greater is He who is in me than he who is in the world (1 John 4:4)

I have received the gift of righteousness and reign as a king in life by Jesus Christ (Romans 5:17)

I have received the spirit of wisdom and revelation in the knowledge of Jesus, the eyes of my understanding being enlightened (Ephesians 1:17-18)

I have received the power of the Holy Spirit to lay hands on the sick and see them recover, to cast out demons, to speak with new tongues. I have power over all the power of the enemy and nothing shall by any means harm me (Mark 16:17-18; Luke 10:17, 19)

I have put off the old man and have put on the new man, which is renewed in the knowledge after the image of Him who created me (Colossians 3:9-10)

I have given and it is given to me; good measure, pressed down, shaken together, and running over, men give into my bosom [life] (Luke 6:38)

I have no lack for my God supplies all of my need according to His riches in glory by Christ Jesus (Philippians 4:19)

I can quench all the fiery darts of the wicked one with my shield of faith (Ephesians 6:16)

I can do all things through Christ Jesus (Philippians 4:13)

I shall do even greater works than Christ Jesus (John 14:12)

I show forth the praises of God who has called me out of darkness into His marvelous light (1 Peter 2:9)

I am God's child – for I am born again of the incorruptible seed of the Word of God, which lives and abides forever (1 Peter 1:23)

I am God's workmanship, created in Christ unto good works (Ephesians 2:10)

I am a new creature in Christ (1 Corinthians 5:17)

I am a spirit being – alive to God (1 Thessalonians 5:23; Romans 6:11)

I am a believer and the light of the Gospel shines in my mind (II Corinthians 4:4)

I am a doer of the Word and blessed in my actions (James 1:22,25)

I am a joint-heir with Christ (Romans 8:17)

I am more than a conqueror through Him who loves me (Romans 8:37)

I am an overcomer by the blood of the Lamb and the word of my testimony (Revelation 12:11)

I am a partaker of His divine nature (II Peter 1:3,4)

I am an ambassador for Christ (II Corinthians 5:20)

I am part of a chosen generation, a royal priesthood, a holy nation, a purchased people (I Peter 2:9)

I am the righteousness of God in Jesus Christ (II Corinthians 5:21)

I am the temple of the Holy Spirit; I am not my own (I Corinthians 6:19)

I am the head and not the tail; I am above only and not beneath (Deuteronomy 28:13)

I am the light of the world (Matthew 5:14)

I am His elect, full of mercy, kindness, humility, and longsuffering (Romans 8:33; Colossians 3:12)

I am forgiven of all my sins and washed in the Blood (Ephesians 1:7)

I am delivered from the power of darkness and translated into God's kingdom (Colossians 1:13)

I am redeemed from the curse of sin, sickness, and poverty (Galatians 3:13; Deuteronomy 28:15-68)

I am firmly rooted, built up, established in my faith and overflowing with gratitude (Colossians 2:7)

I am called of God to be the voice of His praise (II Timothy 1:9; Psalm 66:8)

I am healed by the stripes of Jesus (I Peter 2:24; Isaiah 53:5)

I am raised up with Christ and seated in heavenly places (Colossians 2:12; Ephesians 2:6)

I am greatly loved by God (Colossians 3:12, Romans 1:7; 1 Thessalonians 1:4; Ephesians 2:4)

I am strengthened with all might according to His glorious power (Colossians 1:11)

I am submitted to God and the devil flees from me because I resist him in the Name of Jesus (James 4:7)

I press on toward the goal to win the prize to which God in Christ Jesus is calling us upward (Philippians 3:14)

For God has not given us a spirit of fear; but of power, love, and a sound mind (II Timothy 1:7)

It is not I who live, but Christ lives in me (Galatians 2:20)

~~~~~~~~~~~~~~~~~~~~~~~~~~~~~~~~

Psalm 91 - *Personalized*

I, *[Insert your name here]*, who lives in the shelter of the Most High,

Will find rest in the shadow of the Almighty.

This I declare of the Lord:

He alone is my refuge, my place of safety;

He is my God, and I trust Him.

For He will rescue me from every trap

And protect me from the fatal plague,

He will shield me with His wings.

He will shelter me with His Feathers.

His faithful promises are my armor and

213

protection.

I will not be afraid of the terrors of night,

Nor fear the dangers of the day,

Nor dread the plague that stalks in darkness,

Nor the disaster that strikes at midday.

Though a thousand fall at my side,

Though ten thousand are dying around me,

These evils will not touch me.

But I will see it with my eyes;

I will see how the wicked are punished.

If I make the Lord my refuge,

If I make the Most High my shelter,

No evil will conquer me;

No plague will come near my dwelling.

For He orders His angels

To protect me wherever I go.

They will hold me with their hands

To keep me from striking my foot on a stone.

I will trample down lions and poisonous snakes;

I will crush fierce lions and serpents under my feet!

The Lord says, "I will rescue you, *[Insert your name here]*, who loves me.

I will protect you because you trust in My Name.

When you call on Me, I will answer you;

I will be with you in trouble.

I will rescue you and honor you.

I will satisfy you with a long life

And give you my Salvation."

~~~~~~~~~~~~~~~~~~~~~~~~~~~~~

Letter from God

I received this as a printed copy from a person identified only as anonymous.

To My Precious *[Use Son or Daughter]* *[Insert your name here]*:

Because I knew even before I created the earth that you would accept My love for you, and that you would seek to know Me thus…

In the beginning I created the heavens and the earth.

Then at the right time and in the right place I created you. I created your inner most being, I created every part of you, I knit you together in your mother's womb. You were carefully and wonderfully made; my works are wonderful, and you *[Insert your name here]* are my work. My eyes saw your unformed body. All the days planned for you were written in my book before one of them came to be. How precious are my thoughts for you, How great is the number of them! If you were to count them, they would outnumber the grains of sand.

Listen to me; *[Insert your name here]* I created you and have cared for you since before you were born. I will be your God throughout your lifetime, until your hair is white with age. I made you, and I will care for you. I will carry you along and save you. I will carry you in my arms, holding you close to my heart. For I know the plans that I have for you plans to prosper you and not to harm you, plans to give you hope and a future.

[Insert your name here] there are some times of suffering in your life. But the temporary suffering of this life does not compare to the glory that shall be revealed in you. Know this that I am with you and I will help you. Your help comes from me, I am the God who created the heavens and the earth, and the one who created you. I will never leave you, I will never reject you. When your parents fail you I will pick you up, hold you close, and adopt you. Nothing can ever separate you from my love for you. When you are in trouble and distress my love is

with you. When you are persecuted my love is with you. When you are hungry and cold and naked my love is with you, I am always with you. When you are in danger and threatened with death my love is with you, I will be with you forever.

[Insert your name here] know that nothing can separate you from my love, no matter how high you go, no matter how deep you sink, nothing in life and not even death can separate you from Me, and My love for you. No demon or any other power in hell can separate you from my love. My love for you is revealed through Christ Jesus your Lord. In all things and every situation you will have victory, you will conquer, because the victory of Christ Jesus is your victory.

But now, *[Insert your name here]*, I the LORD, who created you and formed you, says: Do not be afraid, for I have purchased you, I have called you by name; you are mine. When you go through deep waters and great trouble, I will be with you. When you go through rivers of difficulty, they will not over flow you. When you walk through the fire, you will not be burned. I command you to be strong and courageous! Do not be afraid; do not be dismayed, for I, the LORD your God will be with you everywhere you go.

[Insert your name here], know that everything will work together for your good, because you love me. You have been called according to my purpose. For I knew you before you were born and I predestined you to be

conformed to the likeness of my Son, Jesus Christ. This is your destiny, and this is your purpose, that you become one with my Son Jesus, and thus one with me. I created you in my image so that you and I can express love to each other. The most intimate relationship you can have is with me because you and I are becoming one. You and your brothers and sisters that believe in me are becoming one with Jesus, and thus one with me. You in me, and me in you, together, unified by my love for you. You were designed for this purpose, nothing else will ever satisfy your deepest needs, you deepest desires, only I can. Because you seek to know me I satisfy your heart with love, joy, and peace that only I can give you.

[Insert your name here], if you should forget me, and enter into sin, and not turn back to Me on your own then I will punish you. Because your sin will separate you from feeling My presence, and My influence, and I want you to return to your first love, the One who loves you. I the Lord discipline those I love, and punish everyone who I accept as my child. Just as a good Father disciplines His children to turn them away from a dangerous path, so I shall discipline you for your good, that you may share in My holiness. No discipline seems pleasant at the time, but painful. Later on, however, it produces a harvest of righteousness and peace for those who have been trained by it.

[Insert your name here], do not forget all my benefits, I forgive all your sins and heal all your diseases, I rescue

your life from the pit of destruction and crown you with love and compassion. I satisfy your desires with good things so that your youth is renewed like the eagles. I The Lord work righteousness and justice for all the oppressed; I The Lord am compassionate and gracious, slow to anger, abounding in love. I will not always accuse, nor will I harbor my anger forever, I do not treat you as your sins deserve or repay you according to your iniquities. For as high as the heavens are above the earth, so great is My love for you because you fear Me; as far as the east is from the west, so far have I removed your transgressions from you.

[Insert your name here], call to Me, and I will answer you, and show you great and mighty things, which you do not know. Always pray to Me about your every concern, pray from your mouth and pray from your heart, I hear every thought that you think. Everything that you care about, I care about also because it concerns you. Cast all your cares and anxiety on Me because I love you. Trust in Me, the LORD YOUR GOD, with all your heart, do not depend on your own understanding; In everything acknowledge Me, and I will direct your paths. Do not worry about anything, but in everything big or small, by prayer, with thanksgiving, present your requests to Me, the Most High God. And I will give you My peace in your heart, peace that is beyond all human understanding, and it will guard your heart and your mind in Christ Jesus. Always be joyful. Keep on praying always. No matter what happens, always be thankful, for this is My will for

you because you belong to Me.

[Insert your name here], Study My Book of law and truth, the Holy Bible, do not let My words depart from your mouth; meditate on it day and night, so that you may be careful to do everything written in it. Then you will be prosperous and successful. My words are Spirit and they are Life. If you remain in me and my words remain in you, ask whatever you will, and it will be given you. For the word of God is living and powerful. Sharper than any double-edged sword, it penetrates even to dividing soul and spirit, joints and marrow; it judges the thoughts and attitudes of the heart. The most important thing you will ever own is your Bible because it gives you knowledge of Me, The Most High God. It makes the poor rich, it gives hope to the hopeless, faith to the fearful, food to the hungry, water to the thirsty, love to the despised, comfort to the lonely, freedom to the prisoner, health to the sick, light in the darkness, and life to the dying.

[Insert your name here], I have set up circumstances and situations in your life to cause you to seek Me and find Me. I desire that you know Me. I am the Lord your God, full of compassions, and gracious, slow to anger, abounding in love and faithfulness. Let not the wise man glory in his wisdom, Let not the mighty man glory in his might, Nor let the rich man glory in his riches; But *[Insert your name here]* glory in this, That you understand and know Me, That I am the LORD, exercising compassion, loving-kindness, judgment, and

righteousness in the earth. For in these I delight and take pleasure.

All things are created for My pleasure and My pleasure is to show forth loving compassion. I have compassion on the poor and needy, and I am a Father to the fatherless, I help them, and I defend them. Far below Me are the heavens and the earth, I stoop to look down, and I lift the poor from the dirt and the needy from the garbage dump and I set them among princes. *[Insert your name here]*, I want you to do these things also, have compassion on the poor and needy and help them, this is what it means to know Me. For I am Love, and when you live in love, you live in Me, and I live in you. Loving compassion is good, and this is what I require from you, to do what is right, to love compassion, and to walk humbly with your God.

As a father has compassion on his children, so I your LORD have compassion on you because you fear Me; for I know how you were formed, I remember that you are dust. Forever and ever My love is with you because you fear Me, and My righteousness with your children's children; with those who keep My covenant and remember to obey My laws. My law is to love. You shall love the LORD your God with all your heart, with all your soul, and with all your mind. This is the first and great commandment. And the second is like it: You shall love your neighbor as yourself. On these two commandments all of My laws are based. When you walk in love you are obeying all My laws. When you walk in Love you are walking in My Holy Spirit for I AM LOVE!

[Insert your name here], come and live in My shelter, in the protection of the Most High God, you will find rest in the presence of the Almighty. You will say, "This I declare of the LORD: He alone is my refuge, my place of safety; He is my God, and I am trusting Him." *[Insert your name here]*, I will rescue you from every trap and protect you from the fatal plague. I will shield you with My wings. I will shelter you with My feathers. My faithful promises are your armor and protection. Do not be afraid of the terrors of the night, nor fear the dangers of the day, nor dread the plague that stalks in darkness, nor the disaster that strikes at midday. Though a thousand fall at your side, though ten thousand are dying around you, these evils will not touch you. But you will see it with your eyes; you will see how the wicked are punished.

Because you, *[Insert your name here]*, make the LORD your refuge, because you make the Most High your shelter, no evil will conquer you; no plague will come near your dwelling. For I order My angels to protect you wherever you go. They will hold you with their hands to keep you from striking your foot on a stone. You will trample down lions and poisonous snakes; you will crush fierce lions and serpents under your feet!

[Insert your name here], My servant, and My friend, whom I have chosen, I have chosen you and have not rejected you. So do not fear, for I am with you; do not be

dismayed, for I am your God. I will strengthen you and help you; I will hold you up with my righteous right hand. All who come against you will surely be ashamed and disgraced; those who oppose you will be as nothing and perish. Though you search for your enemies, you will not find them. Those who wage war against you will be as nothing at all. For I am the LORD, your God, who takes hold of your right hand and says to you, do not fear; I will help you. Do not be afraid, for I myself will help you declares the LORD, your Redeemer. You will rejoice in the LORD and glory in the Holy One of Israel.

[Insert your name here], when you asked Me to forgive your sins and come into your heart I sent My Holy Spirit into you to comfort you, to give you power, and as proof to you that I have adopted you as My child. The Holy Spirit shall lead you into all truth because He shall testify of Jesus, and He will give you power to testify of Jesus. I will speak to you through My Holy Spirit that is in you, He will tell you what is right and wrong, what is love and hate. My Holy Spirit is a gentle whisper inside your heart telling you the path to walk in. If you walk in My Spirit you will walk in love, you will not sin. And you will see great and mighty things happen before you, they will not be accomplished by strength, nor by outside force, but by My Spirit says the LORD ALMIGHTY. Through My Holy Spirit I shall give you supernatural gifts that you may be blessed, and that you shall bless others through demonstrating My love for them. My Holy Spirit will be with you through out your whole life, and after I receive

you into My glory.

I your LORD say to you I will rescue you because you love me. I will protect you because you trust in my name. When you call on me, I will answer; I will be with you in trouble. I will rescue you and honor you. I will satisfy you with a long life and give you my salvation. Call upon Me in the day of trouble; I will deliver you, and you shall glorify Me. It is your destiny.

Thus Says THE LORD Your GOD!

~~~~~~~~~~~~~~~~~~~~~~~~~

Miscellaneous Statements

I spend quality time in meditation and prayer every day

I listen for and recognize the voice of my Lord Jesus

I obey my Lord's voice

I have an intimate relationship with Jesus

I trust the Lord completely

I realize that Jesus is my best friend and constant companion

I find comfort, peace, reassurance, safety, and calmness in my Lord's presence

I grow closer to Jesus everyday

My Lord Jesus is loving, kind, patient, tolerant, gentle, strong, considerate, merciful, all wise, all knowing, all powerful, protective of me, rescues me, counsels me, guides me, accepts me and loves me completely exactly as I am today in this moment.

Jesus is always right beside me wherever I go and whatever I do.

Jesus has a wonderful sense of humor

Jesus fills me and my life with Joy and Laughter

Jesus feels everything I feel

Jesus wants me to be happy and whole

Jesus wants the best for me

Jesus wants me to live a long healthy and happy life

My Lord Jesus has a good reason for everything that has happened or will happen in my life

God has forgiven me for my past and future mistakes

God has set me free through the death of His Son Jesus Christ

God always has my best interests at heart

God has a wonderful plan for my life

I am a channel of God's love and power to everyone I

meet

When faced with indecision or a challenge in my life I rely on the Holy Spirit in me to guide me and direct me in the choice or action that He would have me to take

I always remember that the Lord has a reason for everything that happens

The Lord is my top priority at all times

The Lord blesses and prospers me in all that I do

I express my gratitude to the Lord on a daily basis for all He has done and will do in my life

I am in awe of the Lord's majesty and power

I am grateful for the Lord's tenderness and everlasting patience with me

I reflect the Lord's love and personality in all that I do

I honor the Lord with my mind and my heart

I glorify the Lord with my actions and words

The Lord uses my mouth, hands, and feet to touch other's lives

I will continually praise the Lord for His Mercy and Kindness

I study the Word of God and pray for others everyday

Section 5:
PTSD AND/ OR MENTAL ILLNESS AFFIRMATIONS

Note:

These are examples from my personal recording. I strongly recommend that if you have PTSD and/or a mental illness, you review this section with your Therapist or Counselor before recording to come up with your own personalized list according to your specific needs. Where there are a group of words in parenthesis ( ), pick the one word that fits your life.

On my recording, I read through this section at least twice, in order to maximize the messages to my brain. This process worked to drastically reduce the intensity and frequency of flashbacks and nightmares that I experienced.

~~~~~~~~~~~~~~~~~~~~~~~~~~~~~~~~

227

I keep all my appointments with my Mental Health Professionals and I arrive on time

I see my (Psychiatrist, Psychologist, Therapist, or Counselor) on a regular basis

I am open and honest with my (Psychiatrist, Psychologist, Therapist, or Counselor) regarding all areas of my life

I follow all directions given by my (Psychiatrist, Psychologist, Therapist, or Counselor) to the letter

I take all of my prescribed medication as I am directed to do by my Psychiatrist

I take my medication in the proper amounts as directed by my Psychiatrist

I freely discuss any concerns I have about my medications with my Psychiatrist

When I decide that I want to be medication free, I will make a plan with my Psychiatrist to achieve that goal and follow the plan as laid out

I fully participate in my Therapy group realizing that the more involved I am, the more beneficial it will be to my overall mental health

I am surrounded by positive and caring friends

I live life one moment at a time

My thoughts remain focused on today

When I notice my body becoming anxious, I immediately focus on relaxing and deep breathing

When I feel myself becoming stressed, I immediately focus my mind on calming thoughts, I purposely relax and practice deep breathing

When I feel overwhelmed, I remind myself that the longest journey is accomplished by one step at a time and I focus on doing and completing one thing at a time

I attend all of my support groups and meetings on time

I contribute to my support groups and meetings in a confident manner by sharing my thoughts and my time

I see myself as a valuable and worthy person

Each day I grow stronger and healthier mentally and emotionally

I call and speak with another member of my support group ever day

When I find my mind reliving past events, I immediately bring myself back to the present moment, noticing everything around me in this moment, reminding myself that I am safe, healthy, and whole.

If I find myself in mental and/or emotional pain of any kind, I immediately pick up the phone and call someone. If no one answers, I call another person and keep calling until I reach someone to talk to.

When someone asks me how I am doing, I reply honestly instead of saying, "I'm fine."

I do something good for myself everyday

I do something I enjoy everyday

I value the people in my life and tell them or show them how much I value them often

I have a gratitude list and read it everyday

I treat myself with respect and honor

I treat others with respect and honor

I practice healthy boundaries in all areas of my life

When I notice an unhealthy behavior in my life, I immediately replace it with a healthy behavior

I focus on the positive in myself and in others

When I feel overwhelmed by my past experiences, I refocus my mind on my present surroundings

When I feel the walls closing in on me, I close my eyes and practice slow deep breathing. I focus my mind on a beautiful meadow filled with soft green grass, a brilliant blue sky with soft puffy white clouds, and a gentle summer breeze softly brushing against my skin. I hold this picture in my mind and continue deep breathing until I feel calm and peaceful.

As I begin to fall asleep, I allow only positive and comforting thoughts to enter my mind. If any negative or ugly thoughts come into my mind, I immediately see myself pushing those thoughts into a hole in the ground and snapping the cover down over that hole tightly. As I secure that cover, I know that those thoughts are gone forever and cannot hurt me.

As I am falling asleep, my body relaxes and breathing becomes deeper and slower

As I am falling asleep, I am safe and protected by God's angels

I sleep deeply and peacefully

I dream of being surrounded by loving and supportive people

I dream of sweet and beautiful scenes and places

I dream of joyful times filled with laughter and surrounded by good friends

Section 6:
ADDICTION RECOVERY AFFIRMATIONS

The affirmations and positive statements in this section can be adapted to fit recovery in any 12-step program. I highly recommend that you refer to your recovery program's specific literature as a source for additional affirmations to add to this section of your recording. For example, if you attend Al-Anon meetings for families and friends of alcoholics, you could use the ODAT (One Day At A Time) book. This book has a daily reading and meditation for every day of the year. Another good source is your sponsor or spiritual advisor.

~~~~~~~~~~~~~~~~~~~~~~~~~~~~~~~~~~~~~

I am free from the desire to (use, participate in, etc.) (describe addiction, i.e. alcohol, drugs, gambling, sex, etc.)

I participate fully in my recovery everyday

I call my sponsor everyday

I talk to another person in my recovery program everyday in addition to calling my sponsor

I attend meetings (number of times) per week
I arrive at all of my meetings at least 15 minutes early and remain for at least 15 minutes after the meeting has ended

I introduce myself to someone new at every meeting and ask how they are doing with sincerity and concern

I help in setting up the meeting rooms and/or cleaning up after the meetings

I fully participate in meetings when asked to do so or when called upon

I respect the time limits when asked to speak or share in a meeting

I volunteer to participate in being of service in my recovery program such as leading meetings or serving on committees

I encourage newcomers by offering them a handshake and a word of encouragement and support

I read at least one paragraph of (name of recover literature, i.e. big book, NA book, etc.) everyday

I work the 12 steps with a sponsor on a regular basis

I respect the 12 traditions and follow them to the best of my ability

I respect other people's anonymity by keeping their name and their attendance at meetings to myself

I choose to remain free of the practice of or the temptation to participate in gossip and/or rumors

I am honest in all areas of my life

I make amends as soon as I realize I have offended anyone

I participate in prayer and meditation every day

When I am tempted to return to my addiction, I immediately call someone in recovery and go directly to a meeting, sharing my thoughts of relapse

I am free from selfish concerns

I am free from self-centered behavior

I practice acceptance in all areas of my life

When I feel anxious or upset, I immediately focus my mind on things that make me feel calm and serene

I journal disturbing thoughts and feelings everyday, knowing that as I write them down I am releasing their power over my mind and emotions

I remind myself that there are times when the best amends I can make is to be a productive and caring member of society, giving to those around me

I choose to live in courage and leave fear behind me

Section 7:
TEENAGE AFFIRMATIONS

Living through the teenage years is perhaps one of the most difficult times of life for some of us. Hormones cause emotions to go on a rollercoaster ride. The intense desire to be liked and accepted by peers becomes most important. The struggle to find an independent identity apart from the parent-child relationship can become a love-hate relationship. Parents are often frustrated and angry because they do not know how to respond to your needs. You feel angry and frustrated because you don't know how to tell them what you need, but you know you love them. There is no easy answer or quick fix, but helping yourself to develop a positive core belief about yourself can help.

I wish someone had given me a set of affirmations and positive statements to record and listen to everyday. It would have made the transition toward adulthood easier and my reactions to teenage life less painful.

Use this section in addition to the previous sections. Cover each area of your life as outlined in Section 3 to maximize your results.

As previously stated, these examples are just suggestions. Create affirmations and positive statements that apply to you, your life, your dreams and goals. Remember to avoid the negative words and do not use them for relationships in dating others (see personal warning in Chapter 4).

I am beautiful inside and out

I am intelligent

I am creative and talented

I am free of fear and insecurity

I am happy and at peace inside

I live in the moment and enjoy the beauty around me

I am healthy spiritually, mentally, emotionally, and physically

I am strong and resilient

I am persistent and press toward the goal of success

I am intuitive and insightful

I trust my gut feelings to guide me in all situations

I pay attention to my gut feelings, knowing that if I feel something is wrong, it is

I pay attention to my gut feelings and choose to follow its warnings to avoid getting myself or others in trouble or in a dangerous situation

I am careful and consider my choices

I am thoughtful and wise

I am self-confident and self-assured

I am loving and kind to all people and God's creatures

I am free from worry and anxiety

I am free from the need to impress others

Before taking any action, I consider the results and possible consequences of my actions

I am free from the need to gossip about others

I am honest and truthful

I respect authority

I use good manners with all people

I respect my elders

I am compassionate and caring

I feel empathy for those who suffer and are less fortunate

than I am

I choose constructive action in place of destructive action

When I feel angry, I immediately stop and breathe deeply, forcing myself to relax and think about the cause of my anger

When I feel angry, I choose my actions carefully, knowing that any action or reaction can affect me for the rest of my life

When I feel angry, I immediately make myself do something positive like going for a run, exercising, or practicing a sport to release my emotion

When I feel sad or lonely, I call a friend or write in a journal to release the power of my emotions

When I feel sad or lonely, I make a gratitude list, writing at least 10 things I am grateful for in my life

When I feel sad or lonely, I watch a comedy to make myself laugh

When I feel sad or lonely, I force myself to think positive and take positive action

When I make a mistake, I immediately forgive myself and remind myself that I am human, everyone makes mistakes and it is not the end of my world

When I make a mistake, I immediately learn the lesson of

the experience without beating myself up about it and I move on to something positive

I am beautiful inside and out

I know and understand that I am a worthy person exactly as I am in this moment

I accept myself completely in this moment, exactly as I am now

I am self-confident

I choose to value my own opinion first, in place of letting others define who I am

I accept that friends will come and go in my life

I know that if I lose one best friend, I will find another

I choose my friends wisely

I choose my peer group wisely, knowing that the type of friends I surround myself with defines my identity

I choose my friends and peer group wisely, knowing that the seeds I plant in my life today follow me and define my future tomorrow

I choose to keep moving forward in my life

I choose to see failure as a learning process that brings me one step closer to success

I accept my parents for who they are now

I realize that even when communication with my parents becomes difficult, they love me and want the best for me

I love and respect my parents

I choose to value who I am in this moment

I choose to see myself as someone with an awesome future ahead of me

I make decisions that contribute to my success in every area of my life

I choose to drink water, tea, or soda in place of alcohol

I choose to practice healthy living in all areas of my life

I choose to be free of all chemicals

I only drink or eat things that add to my spiritual, mental, emotional, and physical health

I am a channel of love, laughter, and joy

I am a bright shining light in the darkness

I am supportive and encouraging to those around me

I focus on positive thoughts continually

I add to this world in place of taking from it

Section 8:
NOTE PAGES

The following pages are included to give you a working area as you read through the book. You can take notes or begin writing your affirmations and positive statements script.

Another use for these pages is to note any text from another book or source here so that when you are ready to record, you don't have to search in other places.

You can also use this area as a place to note questions or topics you would like to research.

NOTE PAGES

NOTE PAGES

Illustrations

1. Business Lady Writing On Notebook by adamr, Free Digital
   Photos.net
   http://www.freedigitalphotos.net/images/Computing_g36
   8-Business_Lady_Writing_On_Notebook_p98730.html

About the Author

Georganne Bickle is a Native Phoenician and a veteran of the AZ Air National Guard, U.S. Air Force, and U.S. Navy. Her heritage includes Italian, German, and Choctaw with current membership in the Choctaw Nation of Oklahoma. She graduated from Phoenix College with an Associate of Arts Degree in 2008 and graduated from Regent University with a Bachelor of Arts Degree in 2012. She self-published her first book *Dear Men: A True Story* in 2008. Her previous experience included working as an Extra/Background in Commercials, Television Shows, and Films, along with performing stand-up comedy on the amateur circuit in the Los Angeles and Phoenix metro areas. Her background includes over twenty years of working as a volunteer counselor with women in recovery, as well as current sobriety of nearly seventeen years. She has successfully learned to manage and overcome: PTSD, Bipolar, Military and Civilian Sexual Traumas, Alcoholism, and Smoking by surrounding herself with a strong support system, regular church attendance, and an ongoing recovery program. Her healing and recovery has been dramatically enhanced by the daily use of a personalized recording for the past ten years.

Other Books by Georganne Bickle

Dear Men: A True Story, pub. 2008

Collection of Military Short Stories,
in process

Silent Heroes: The forgotten men of Guadalcanal
in process

Military Property: A Survivor's Story
in process